Grammar, Punctuation & Style: A Quick Guide for Lawyers and Other Writers

Deborah Cupples
Senior Legal Skills Professor
University of Florida
Levin College of Law

Margaret Temple-Smith
Senior Legal Skills Professor
University of Florida
Levin College of Law

WEST®

© 2013 LEG, Inc. d/b/a West Academic Publishing

610 Opperman Drive
St. Paul, MN 55123
1-800-313-9378

Printed in the United States of America
ISBN: 978-0-314-28807-3

MAT: 41455349

Book Design: Carol Dungan Logie

TABLE OF CONTENTS

ACKNOWLEDGEMENTS

FOR EDITORIAL or research-related assistance, we are grateful to the following:

- Pam Chandler
- Cami Cupples
- Hanna Edeback
- Emily Frazier
- Louis Higgins
- Laura Holle
- Bonnie Karlen
- Gregory Kwok
- Ron Kozlowski
- Carol Logie
- Dr. Wayne Losano
- Prof. Lynn LoPucki
- Peg O'Connor
- Greg Olson
- William P. Reynolds
- Melissa Rider
- Dr. Kendra Siler-Marsiglio
- Nicholas Temple-Smith
- Katherine Thomason
- Prof. Diane Tomlinson
- Joy Wilcox
- Nancy Wilcox

For other forms of help or support, we are grateful to the following:

Caroline Moss Emanuel; Victorina Basauri; William Cupples; Dr. Gustavo Antonini; Nancy Baldwin; Susan Carr; Larry Keith Southerland, Esq.; Christine M. Morris; Dr. Kent N. Wenger; and our colleagues and staff at the University of Florida's Levin College of Law, including Fletcher Baldwin, Anne Rutledge, Gaylin Soponis, Leslie Knight, Sylvia Menendez, Karen Kays, and the Legal Writing faculty.

Grammar, Punctuation & Style:

A Quick Guide for Lawyers and Other Writers

CHAPTER 1.
Some Basics About Grammar

I. THE IMPORTANCE OF GOOD GRAMMAR

GOOD GRAMMAR IS IMPORTANT because (1) it promotes clarity and (2) people whose opinions matter might judge you based on your grammar. Yes, some employers actually might toss an applicant's materials into the wastebasket after spotting errors in a résumé.

Whatever type of writing you do, your credibility is at risk if your grammar is bad. Why risk losing face—or losing an opportunity—when it is so easy to get the grammar and punctuation right? To understand certain rules of grammar and punctuation, you must understand certain grammatical terms, which are discussed in Section II.

We recommend that you keep your grammar handbook nearby when you write or edit. If it is not handy, you could check online resources such as *Grammar Girl* (Mignon Fogarty), *Grammar Handbook* (University of Illinois), or *Lynch's Guide to Grammar and Style* (Rutgers University).

Note for Lawyers: Courts have consulted grammar handbooks when construing legal documents[1]—in some cases, multiple handbooks.[2] In addition to this book, we recommend that you get at least one other handbook because courts tend to prefer support from multiple sources. Given that courts sometimes use grammatical terms when construing legal text,[3] a lawyer who is not familiar with such terms is at a disadvantage.

II. REFRESHER: SOME KEY GRAMMATICAL TERMS

A. The Eight Parts of Speech

There are eight parts of speech in modern English.

Eight Parts of Speech

• Noun	• Verb	• Conjunction
• Pronoun	• Adverb	• Interjection
• Adjective	• Preposition	

A **noun** names a person or other life form, a place, a thing, or an idea. Nouns have case (subjective, objective, possessive—though the form changes for only the possessive). Nouns also express number (singular or plural).

EXAMPLES: **Nouns**

• William	• house	• car	• hope
• judge	• Iowa	• apple	• justice
• dog	• Tampa	• water	• chaos

A **pronoun** refers to or acts as a substitute for a noun. Like nouns, pronouns have case and express number (pronoun case is discussed in Section IV).

EXAMPLES: **Pronouns**

I	you	he/she/it
we	yourself	they
us	yours	them

The noun to which a pronoun refers is called the **antecedent**.

EXAMPLES: **Antecedents**
(bold antecedent, underlined pronoun)

- I paid **the lawyer** after <u>she</u> drafted my contract.
- **Bill** gave <u>his</u> money to a charity.

An **adjective** describes or modifies a noun or pronoun. **Articles** (e.g., *a, an, the*) are a subclass of adjectives.

EXAMPLES: **Adjectives Modifying Nouns**

- <u>Big</u> car
- <u>New</u> house
- <u>Vague</u> statute
- <u>Complex</u> contract

♦ Verbs, Adverbs

A **verb** signifies action or state of being. A verb may consist of one or more words. Verbs show timing (e.g., past, present, future).

EXAMPLES: **Verbs**

is	was	will be
have	had	will have
is reading	was reading	will be reading

An **adverb** describes or modifies a verb, an adjective, another adverb, or a clause. Many adverbs end in *–ly*, but some do not.

EXAMPLES: **Adverbs**

- Emily writes <u>well</u>.
  [Adverb *well* modifies the verb *writes*.]

- The contract was <u>fairly</u> complete.
  [Adverb *fairly* modifies the adjective *complete*.]

- Anne did the job <u>very</u> thoroughly.
  [Adverb *very* modifies the adverb thoroughly, which modifies the verb *did*.]

A **preposition** shows the relationship between words, phrases or clauses.

> **EXAMPLES: Prepositions in a Sentence**
>
> • Cami is studying <u>at</u> the university.
> • Katie walked <u>toward</u> Greg.
> • The plaintiff was driving <u>on</u> a public road.
> • The dispute was <u>about</u> the insurance policy.

Often, prepositions show the position (in time or space) of one thing in relation to another. The following is a partial list of **common prepositions**.

about	except	since
above	for	than
across	from	through
around	in	to
before	into	toward
behind	like	under
between	near	until
by	of	up
down	over	with
during	regarding	within

A **conjunction** connects (or conjoins) words, phrases, or clauses.

EXAMPLES: **Conjunctions**

- She wants <u>apples</u> **or** <u>oranges</u>.
  [*connecting two words*]
- The writer sought <u>a literary agent</u> **and**
  <u>a good lawyer</u>.
  [*connecting two phrases*]
- <u>Scott waited for the shipment</u>, **but** <u>it was late</u>.
  [*connecting two clauses*]

An **interjection** can introduce a remark or express emotion (e.g., joy, surprise, resignation). Interjections are rarely appropriate in legal, business, or technical writing but do have a place in some other types of writing (e.g., fiction).

EXAMPLES: **Interjections**

- **Hey,** where are you going to eat lunch?
- **Ah,** that is what she meant.
- **Yes!** I won the lottery.
- **Oh no!** I've been robbed.

We recommend a cautious approach to using interjections (especially with an exclamation point, which can be distracting).

Some words—such as *that*—can be used as different parts of speech, depending on the context.

EXAMPLE: *That* **Used as Different Parts of Speech**

- Adjective: That dog is vicious.
- Adverb: It didn't cost that much money.
- Conjunction: She knew that Joe was right.
- Pronoun: That is the Plaintiff's property.

B. Other Key Grammatical Terms

A **sentence** is a set of words that expresses a complete thought. A sentence must contain at least one subject and one predicate.

A **subject** is a noun or noun substitute about which a sentence says (or asks) something. In a sentence that has only one subject and one verb, the sentence's subject is also the verb's subject.

The **predicate** is what is said (or asked) about a sentence's subject. A predicate must include at least one verb.

EXAMPLES: **Subjects and Predicates**

- Gaylin edited the contract perfectly.
    S   P
- The senator was found guilty of accepting bribes.
         S   P
- The Landlord shall maintain the pool area.
        S   P

A **clause** is a group of related words that contains a subject and a predicate. An *independent clause* can stand alone as a complete sentence, but a *dependent clause* cannot:

- **Independent clause**:   Hanna will write the article.
- **Dependent clause**:   After she finishes eating lunch
- **Combined**:   After she finishes eating lunch, Hanna will write the article.

A **phrase** is a group of related words that acts as a grammatical unit. For example, a noun phrase is a group of words that acts as one noun.

EXAMPLES: **Phrases**
(phrases underlined)

- **Noun phrase:** <u>The tall man</u> walked into a bar.
- **Verb Phrase:** Nick <u>had been writing</u> a novel.
- **Prepositional Phrase:** Annie drove <u>to a store</u>.

An **object** is a noun or noun substitute (e.g., a pronoun or noun phrase) that relates to a preposition or a verb. A preposition requires an object to complete the thought.

> EXAMPLES: **Object of a Preposition**
> (preposition underlined, object bolded)
>
> 1. Leslie walked <u>with</u> **John.**
> 2. Judge Huck went <u>into</u> **the courthouse.**

Sentence 1: Without the preposition's object (*John*), the thought would be incomplete. "Leslie walked with" would leave open the question with whom did Leslie walk?

Sentence 2: Without *the courthouse*, the thought would be incomplete. "Judge Huck went into" would leave open the question into what did Judge Huck go?

Like prepositions, some verbs require an object. There are two types of objects for a verb: direct and indirect. A **direct object** is the noun or noun substitute that receives a verb's action. Put another way, a direct object is the thing (physical or non-physical) to which something is done.

> EXAMPLES: **Direct Objects of a Verb**
> (direct object underlined, verb bolded)
>
> • Tim **threw** <u>a large rock</u>.
>   *(physical)*
> • Therapists **analyze** <u>emotions</u>.
>   *(non-physical)*

An **indirect** object is a noun or noun substitute showing to whom or for whom an action is done. Usually, an indirect object indicates (1) who receives the **direct object** or (2) for whom a **direct object** is acted upon. Thus, you cannot have an indirect object without a direct object. Often, a preposition (e.g., to or for) precedes an indirect object.

EXAMPLES: **Indirect Objects of a Verb**
(indirect object bolded, direct object underlined)

- Marilynn gives <u>money</u> to **charities**.
- Joy bought a <u>gift</u> for **Nancy**.
- The Seller sent the **Buyer** <u>the goods</u>.
  [without a preposition, *to* is implied]

A **modifier** is a word, phrase, or clause that describes (or otherwise modifies) a word, phrase, or clause. Adjectives and adverbs are types of modifiers.

EXAMPLES: **Modifiers**

- **Adjective modifying noun:**
  Sylvia is <u>intelligent</u>.

- **Phrase modifying verb:**
  The man went <u>to three restaurants</u>.

- **Adverb modifying verb:**
  The tenant <u>promptly</u> paid the rent.

- **Clause modifying clause:**
  <u>Because the will is unsigned</u>, it is invalid.

- **Word modifying clause:**
  <u>Admittedly</u>, the lawyer was late for court.

A **gerund** is a word consisting of a verb + *ing*. A gerund functions as a noun.

EXAMPLES: **Gerunds**

- <u>Swimming</u> is fun.
- <u>Keeping</u> a pet is a breach of the lease.
- <u>Being</u> earnest is important.

A **participle** is a word formed from a verb. Among other things, a participle can function (1) as an adjective or (2) as part of a verb phrase. A **present participle** is a verb + *ing*. A **past participle** is usually a verb + *ed* (unless the verb is irregular, such as *awoken, drunk,* and *stood*).

EXAMPLES: **Participles as Adjectives**

- The <u>starving</u> artist sold a painting.
- The police chased the <u>injured</u> defendant.
- The <u>forgotten</u> hero returned.
  [irregular verb]

> EXAMPLES: **Participles as Part of a Verb Phrase**
>
> • Shalini <u>will be teaching</u> this semester.
> • The court <u>had reviewed</u> the record.
> • The student <u>had forgotten</u> the rule.
>   [*irregular verb*]

III. A BIT ABOUT VERBS

A. Transitive Verbs and Voice

A **transitive verb** expresses an action that requires a direct object (a thing being acted upon) to receive the verb's action. Direct objects are discussed in Section II.B.

> EXAMPLES: **Transitive Verbs + Direct Objects**
> (transitive verb bolded, direct object underlined)
>
> • Fletcher **makes** <u>the best crab cakes</u>.
> • The defendant **robbed** <u>banks</u>.

A sentence containing a transitive verb can tell its story from the point of view of the actor *or* of the recipient of the action. Thus, transitive verbs have voice.

In **active voice,** the actor is the subject of the sentence and actively carries out the action expressed by the verb. The usual sequence is *Actor* ⇨ *Action* ⇨ *Recipient of action.*

EXAMPLES: **Active Voice**

- **Preston** <u>punched</u> Victor.
  subject   verb   object
- **The seller** <u>will ship</u> the goods.
  subject   verb   object

Passive voice reverses the story: the thing being acted upon becomes the sentence's subject, and the subject passively sits there being acted upon. The usual sequence is *Recipient* ⇨ *Action* ⇨ *Actor* (if the actor is named).

Passive voice requires (1) a verb that expresses the action and (2) a form of *be,* as the following examples show:

- <u>is</u> loved.
- <u>was</u> loved.
- <u>will be</u> loved.
- <u>has been</u> loved.

♦ Passive Voice, Actor

If named, the actor in a passive-voice sentence usually follows the word *by*.

EXAMPLES: **Passive Voice with Named Actor**
(passive subject bolded, passive verb underlined)

- **Victor** <u>was punched</u> *by* Preston.
  subject   verb   actor
- **The goods** <u>will be shipped</u> *by* the seller.
  subject   verb   actor

In passive voice, even if you omit the actor altogether, the sentence would be still be complete.

EXAMPLES: **Passive Voice without Actor**

- **Victor** <u>was punched</u>.
- **The goods** <u>will be shipped</u>.

Passive voice is not grammatically incorrect, though some people might have been taught that it is. In fact, passive voice can be useful because it allows the writer to state an action's consequence while de-emphasizing (or omitting) the actor. Compare the following pairs of examples:

EXAMPLES: **Using Passive Voice to De-Emphasize the Actor**

1(a) Honey, your Ferrari was totaled. *(passive)*
1(b) Honey, I totaled your Ferrari. *(active)*

2(a) Bribes were taken. *(passive)*
2(b) The client took bribes. *(active)*

Passive voice allows the writer to de-emphasize an actor's responsibility—though passive voice here would not stop "Honey" from figuring out who totaled the Ferrari.

B. Intransitive Verbs (No Voice)

Intransitive verbs can express a state of being, a condition, or an action that does not transfer to a direct object. By definition, an intransitive verb does not take a direct object. Because there is no direct object, intransitive verbs do not have voice.

EXAMPLES: **Intransitive Verbs**
(Status or Condition)

- Diane <u>seems</u> content.
- Pat <u>was</u> happy.
- Henry <u>will be</u> punctual.

♦ Intransitive & Transitive Verbs

EXAMPLES: **Intransitive Verbs (Actions)**

- Mary <u>jogs</u> regularly.
- Leanne <u>swims</u> and <u>runs</u>.
- Tomorrow, the trial <u>will begin</u>.

★ **Common-Error Alert:** the mere presence of a form of *be* (e.g., *is, was, were, will be*) does not necessarily indicate passive voice. Used alone, *be* is intransitive and cannot have voice.

C. Verbs That Can Be Transitive or Intransitive

Some verbs can be transitive or intransitive, depending on how they are used in a sentence.

EXAMPLES: **Verbs That Can Be Intransitive or Transitive**

- Intransitive: The mirror <u>broke</u>.
- Transitive: The queen <u>broke</u> the mirror.

- Intransitive: The relationship <u>ended</u>.
- Transitive: Kendra <u>ended</u> the relationship.

D. Verb Tense

1. The Three or Four Tenses

A verb's **tense** expresses timing. There are three or four tenses—depending on which grammar book you consult, as some books label the progressive as a "tense" and others label it as a "form" [4]:

(1) Simple.

(2) Perfect.

(3) Progressive (a.k.a., "continuous").

(4) Perfect progressive.

Note for Lawyers: Case law shows that verb tense can make a difference in how a court construes text. [5]

2. Simple Tense

The **simple tense** indicates that an action or a state of being occurs or exists in the present, occurred or existed in the past, or will occur or exist in the future.

EXAMPLES: **Simple Tense**

Present: He <u>works</u>.

Past: He <u>worked</u>.

Future: He <u>will work</u>.

---

3. Perfect Tense

The **perfect tense** indicates that an action or state of being is, was, or will be **complete** as of a certain point in time.

EXAMPLES: **Perfect Tense**

Present: She <u>has worked</u> before now.
(act is complete as of the present)

Past: She <u>had worked</u> before last week.
(act was complete as of some past point)

Future: She <u>will have worked</u> by next week.
(act will be complete as of some future point)

---

4. Progressive Tense (or Form)

The **progressive** tense (or form) shows that an action or state of being is, was, or will be **in progress** (i.e., ongoing or continuous).

EXAMPLES: **Simple Progressive**

Present: I <u>am working</u>.

Past: I <u>was working</u>.

Future: I <u>will be working</u>.

---

5. Perfect-Progressive Tense

The **present-perfect progressive** indicates that an action or state of being originated in the past and is in progress at present.

> EXAMPLES: **Present -Perfect Progressive**
>
> - She <u>has been working</u> on the project for one month.
> - They <u>have been working</u> at the job site for six days.

The **past-perfect progressive** indicates that an action or state of being was in progress but no longer is (i.e., was completed in the past).

> EXAMPLES: **Past-Perfect Progressive**
>
> - She <u>had been working</u> on the project for one month when they fired her.
> - They <u>had been working</u> at the job site for six days when the dispute began.

The **future-perfect progressive** indicates that an action or state of being that began at an earlier point will still be in progress in the future.

EXAMPLES: **Future-Perfect Progressive**

- By June 15, she <u>will have been working</u> on the project for one month.

- By January 2018, they <u>will have been working</u> at the job site for five years.

---

6. Progressive versus Passive

Many people confuse the progressive tense with passive voice because of the presence of a form of *be* (e.g., *is, was, has been*). Actually, various forms of *be* are used to form some verbs that are not in passive voice.

EXAMPLES: **Form of *Be* but Not Passive Voice**

- Betsy <u>is running</u>.
  [*present progressive, intransitive, no voice*]

- Judge Davis <u>will be reviewing</u> the case.
  [*future progressive, active voice*]

E. Verb Mood

1. Three Moods

A verb can have one of three moods:
- **Indicative**: a statement or question.
- **Imperative:** a command or request (in second person).
- **Subjunctive:** a contrary-to-fact statement.

EXAMPLES: **Verb Moods**

Indicative: Emily helped Jack.
Did Emily help Jack?

Imperative: Emily, go help Jack.

Subjunctive: Jack asked that Emily **help** him.
Jack requested that he **be helped**.

Most people get the indicative and imperative right, so those two moods require no further explanation. For that reason, we devote the rest of this section to the sometimes troublesome subjunctive.

Note for Lawyers: Some courts have discussed a verb's mood when construing legal text.[6]

♦ Subjunctive *Be*

2. The Sometimes Troublesome Subjunctive

a. About the Subjunctive Generally

Verbs in the subjunctive mood express the idea of an action or a state of being that is hypothetical, proposed, supposed, requested, demanded, wished for, or otherwise contrary to fact. The rules for using the subjunctive are unavoidably jargon-rich.[7] The next few subsections discuss the subjunctive uses that tend to be most troublesome.

b. Form of *Be* with *If* or *As Though*

Use *were* instead of *be* (regardless of whether the subject is singular, plural, first person, second person, or third person) in a clause that (1) addresses the present, (2) contains *be*, and (3) begins with *if* or *as though*.

EXAMPLES: **Subjunctive *Be* in a
Present-Tense Clause with *If* or *As Though***

Correct: If I **were** older now, I could retire.

Incorrect: If I <u>was</u> older now, I could retire.

Correct: He struts as though he **were** a rooster.

Incorrect: He struts as though he <u>was</u> a rooster.

In a perfect-tense clause (relating to the past) that begins with *if* or *as though*, use the past-perfect tense.

> EXAMPLES: **Subjunctive *Be* in a
> Perfect-Tense Clause with *If* or *As Though***
>
> **Correct:** If I **had been** at the crime scene
> yesterday, I would have dialed 911.
>
> Incorrect: If I <u>was</u> at the crime scene yesterday,
> I would have dialed 911.
>
> **Correct:** Yesterday, she talked as though she
> **had witnessed** the crime.
>
> Incorrect: Yesterday, she talked as though she
> <u>witnessed</u> the crime.

As though the subjunctive were not confusing enough, not all *if*-clauses take the subjunctive. An *if*-clause expressing something that is **contrary to fact** takes the subjunctive. An *if*-clause expressing something that is **possible** takes the indicative.

◆ Subjunctive and Indicative *If*-Clauses

> EXAMPLES: **Subjunctive and Indicative *If*-Clauses**
>
> • **Subjunctive**
> If I were in law school now, I would be studying.
> [*Contrary to fact: I'm not in law school now.*]
>
> • **Indicative**
> If I get a raise next year, I will be happy.
> [*It's possible that I will get a raise.*]

c. A Request, Demand, or Requirement (with *That*)

In the subjunctive, words expressing a request, demand, or requirement are typically followed by *that*, and the subjunctive is the verb's base form (no ending such as *-ed* or *-s*) regardless of whether the verb is in first, second, or third person.

> EXAMPLES: **Request, Demand or Requirement (with *That*)**
>
> **Correct:** The charity requests that Ben **give** cash.
> Incorrect: The charity requests that Ben gives cash.
>
> **Correct:** The man demanded that the dog **obey**.
> Incorrect: The man demanded that the dog obeys.
>
> **Correct:** The court will require that the jury **leave**.
> Incorrect: The court will require that the jury leaves.

The phrasing is the same as in the previous examples for *asked that, insisted that, proposed that, urged that, suggested that,* and similar constructions.

If the subjunctive verb is a form of *be* on its own, use *be.*

EXAMPLES: **Subjunctive with *Be* on Its Own**

Correct: Victorina asks that Cami **be** on time.

Incorrect: Victorina asks that Cami is on time.

Correct: Dillon will suggest that David **be** ready.

Incorrect: Dillon will suggest that David will be ready.

If the subjunctive verb is a form of *be* plus another verb (if the verb is in passive voice), use *be* with the other verb.

EXAMPLES: **Subjunctive Form of *Be* and Passive Voice**

Correct: Stacey urges that the rule **be enforced**.

Incorrect: Stacey urges that the rule is enforced.

Correct: We will insist that the debt **be paid**.

Incorrect: We will insist that the debt will be paid.

♦ Subjunctive *Be* in a Wish

d. A Wish

When expressing a present wish containing the verb *be*, use *were* (similar to an *if*-clause). When expressing a perfect-tense wish (relating to the past), use the past-perfect tense.

EXAMPLES: Subjunctive *Be* in a Wish

Present Tense

Correct: I wish that I **were** in Key West now.

Incorrect: I wish that I <u>was</u> in Key West now.

Perfect Tense

Correct: Yesterday, I wished that I **had been** in Key West during last year's festival.

Incorrect: Yesterday, I wished that I <u>was</u> in Key West during last year's festival.

IV. A BIT ABOUT PRONOUNS

A. Overview of Pronouns

There are seven types of pronouns: personal, relative, reflexive, intensive, interrogative, demonstrative, and indefinite. This book addresses only the personal, relative, reflexive, and intensive because those are the ones that tend to cause trouble.

B. Pronoun Case

1. The Three Cases

Pronouns can be in one of three cases:

- **Subjective** (or Nominative): <u>I</u> walked.

- **Objective**: John *called* <u>me</u>.

- **Possessive**: The dog was <u>theirs</u>.

The correct case depends on how the pronoun is used.

2. Choosing Between Subjective and Objective Case

Use the **subjective case** if the pronoun is a verb's subject. Use the **objective case** if the pronoun is the object of a verb or preposition.

EXAMPLES: **Subjective (or Nominative) Case**

	Singular	Plural
1st Person	I	We
2nd Person	You	You
3rd Person	He/She/It	They

EXAMPLES: **Objective Case**

	Singular	Plural
1st Person	Me	Us
2nd Person	You	You
3rd Person	Him/Her/It	Them

The choice between the objective and subjective case is fertile ground for error. Most people get it right when a sentence involves one pronoun after a preposition or verb, but multiple objects can be confusing.

You can test whether the case is correct for one of multiple objects by (1) removing any object that is not at issue and (2) reading the sentence with only the pronoun that is at issue.

EXAMPLES: **Objective Versus Subjective Case**

a. Leif went with Rodney and <u>I/me</u>.
  - Is "Leif went with I" correct?
  - No: the preposition *with* takes an object (*me*).

b. Caroline called Maggie and <u>he/him</u>.
  - Is "Caroline called he" correct?
  - No: the transitive verb *called* takes an object (*him*).

Deciding when to use *who* versus *whom* is a question of case. *Who* and *whom* are relative pronouns: they link a relative clause to a main clause by relating back to an antecedent within the main clause.

If the relative pronoun functions as a verb's subject within the relative clause, use the subjective case (*who*). If the relative pronoun functions as an object, use the objective case (*whom*).

Shortcut: try substituting *he* and *him* for the relative pronoun. If *he* is correct, then *who* is correct (*he* and *who* are subjective case). If *him* is correct, then *whom* is correct (*him* and *whom* are objective). It's easy to associate *whom* with *him* because they both end in the letter *m*.

EXAMPLES: **Applying the Who-Whom Shortcut**
(relative clause is underlined)

a. Leland saw the man who/whom hit the car.

- Is "Him hit the car" correct?
- No: the verb "hit" needs a subject (*he*), so *who* is correct.

b. Nancy is a person who/whom people admire.

- Is "people admire he" correct?
- No: the transitive verb *admire* needs an object (*him*), so *whom* is correct.

c. Adam is the man with who/whom she dined.

- Is "she dined with he" correct?
- No: the preposition *with* needs an object (*him*), so *whom* is correct.

---

3. Possessive Case

Use the **possessive case** to indicate ownership (e.g., *my* schedule or *your* book).

EXAMPLES: **Possessive Case**

	Singular	Plural
1st Person	My/Mine	Our/Ours
2nd Person	Your/Yours	Your/Yours
3rd Person	His/Her/Hers/Its	Their/Theirs

★ **Common-Error Alert:** Don't add an apostrophe to a possessive pronoun. It's easy to confuse *its* with *it's*, but they are different words:

- **Its** (possessive pronoun)   The dog bit its tail.
- **It's** (contraction of *it is*)   It's the dog's tail.

Possessive pronouns do not have an apostrophe because the possession is part of the specific pronoun's definition:

- The car was hers. (not *her's*)
- This land is ours. (not *our's*)

C. Pronoun Number and Gender

1. Pronoun Number Agreement

A pronoun must agree in number with its antecedent (i.e., the noun to which the pronoun refers). Use a singular pronoun to refer to a singular antecedent. Use a plural pronoun to refer to a plural antecedent.

★ **Common-Error Alert:** It is incorrect to use *they* or *their* to refer to a singular antecedent.

EXAMPLES: **Pronoun Number Disagreement and Agreement**

Incorrect: A dissatisfied customer may get <u>their</u> money back.

Correct: A dissatisfied customer may get **his or her** money back.

A dissatisfied customer may get **the customer's** money back.

In the example above, *customer* is a singular antecedent, so the pronoun should be singular. Some writers prevent the number-disagreement problem by using *he or she*. Other writers would omit the pronoun and repeat the antecedent.

Writers who prioritize precision over style (e.g., legal, technical, or scientific writers) should consider repeating the antecedent. Writers who strive for an elegant or entertaining style might not want to repeat the antecedent because doing so results in a stiff, pedestrian style.

2. Pronoun Number for Entity or Group

Another common problem relating to pronoun number is the handling of groups or of entities comprised of multiple people. In the U.S., an entity or group is usually treated as singular, so any pronoun referring to an entity or group should also be singular.

EXAMPLES: **Singular Nature of an Entity or Group**

- The **group** made its lunch reservation.
- The **board** will give its members regular updates.
- The **court** reconsidered its order.

---

3. Pronoun Gender Agreement

Pronouns and their antecedents must agree in gender.

EXAMPLES: **Gender-Agreement Rules**

- A feminine antecedent takes a feminine pronoun.
- A masculine antecedent takes a masculine pronoun.
- A neuter antecedent takes a neuter pronoun. (e.g., a corporation or a court is an *it*).

In some contexts, violation of the gender-agreement rule has become a tradition (e.g., sailors refer to a boat as *she*). Gender-neutral writing is further discussed in Chapter 3.

D. Avoiding Ambiguous Pronoun Use

To avoid creating ambiguity, make sure that a pronoun's antecedent (the noun to which the pronoun refers) is clear.

EXAMPLES: **Unclear Antecedents**

- Jessica told Whitney that <u>she</u> was right.
- The doctor plans to see the patient when <u>he</u> returns from vacation.
- When Mac dropped the glass vase onto the glass table, <u>it</u> broke.

Who was right: Jessica or Whitney? Who returns from vacation: the doctor or the patient? What broke: the vase or the table? The easiest way to prevent antecedent-related ambiguity is to omit the pronoun and instead use the antecedent.

EXAMPLES: **Ambiguity Removed through Repetition of Antecedent**

- Jessica told Whitney that <u>Whitney</u> was right.
- The doctor plans to see the patient when <u>the patient</u> returns from vacation.
- When Mac dropped the glass vase onto the glass table, <u>the table</u> broke.

To writers who prioritize style, a repeated antecedent may seem inelegant or dull: those writers might prefer to completely rewrite a sentence containing an ambiguous pronoun.

EXAMPLES: **Ambiguity Removed through Complete Re-writing**

- "You're right," Jessica told Whitney.
- After the patient returns from vacation, the doctor plans to see him.
- The glass table broke when Mac dropped the glass vase onto it.

V. A BIT ABOUT PREPOSITIONS

A. Choosing the Correct Preposition

To write correctly, a writer must choose the correct preposition. You can find examples of correct preposition use in good dictionaries. If looking up the preposition does not give you the answer, try looking up the noun or verb that you are pairing with the preposition. Another option is to search the Internet for the exact phrase that you are considering using (e.g., "susceptible to" and "susceptible of").

While an in-depth discussion of preposition use is beyond this quick guide's scope, the examples in the next few subsections should give you a sense of the importance of correct preposition use.

B. Prepositions in Common Phrases

Some verbs are paired with prepositions. Some verbs are not.

EXAMPLES: **Verbs with and without Prepositions**

- I concurred <u>with</u> her decision.   *(preposition)*
- I dissented <u>from</u> her decision.   *(preposition)*
- I questioned her decision.   *(no preposition)*
- I understood her decision.   *(no preposition)*

Some verbs can go either way (paired with a preposition or not).

EXAMPLES: **Verbs that Can Be Paired with Prepositions or Not**

- I **approved** <u>of</u> her decision.   *(preposition)*
- His supervisor **approved** the plan.   *(no preposition)*
- He **asked** <u>for</u> advice.   *(preposition)*
- She **asked** a question.   *(no preposition)*

◆ Prepositions with Verbs and Nouns

Some verbs can take different prepositions.

EXAMPLES: **Same Verbs with Different Prepositions**

- I asked <u>for</u> the book.
- I asked <u>about</u> the book.
- We paid <u>for</u> the groceries.
- We paid <u>by</u> check (or <u>with</u> a check).

Nouns also may be paired with prepositions to express a specific relationship.

EXAMPLES: **Prepositions Paired with Nouns**

- The **expenditure** <u>of</u> the funds was unauthorized.
- The expenditures <u>for</u> repairs were excessive.
- She expressed **approval** <u>of</u> the project.
- She needed **approval** <u>from</u> the committee.
- The **agreement** <u>with</u> the Buyer fell through.
- The **agreement** <u>of</u> the parties was never signed.

C. Prepositions in Legal Phrases

Some technical phrases that evolved in various professions include prepositions. The following are a few examples from the legal profession:

- A fact may be <u>outside</u> the pleadings.
- A matter may be <u>outside</u> a court's jurisdiction.
- A matter may be <u>within</u> the court's jurisdiction.
- A judge may concur <u>with</u> the majority.
- A judge may dissent <u>from</u> the majority's opinion.
- A party is <u>before</u> a court.
- A lawyer may be rebuked <u>by</u> a court.
- A lawyer may receive a rebuke <u>from</u> a court.

VI. PARALLEL STRUCTURE

A. Parallelism Basics

A list (or series) has **parallel structure** if each list item is grammatically similar. For example, if the first list item is a noun, then the other list items should be nouns. If the first item is a prepositional phrase, then the other list items should be prepositional phrases. Thus, being familiar with the parts of speech (which are discussed in Section II) will help you create parallel structure.

♦ Parallel Structure

EXAMPLE: **Non-Parallel Structure**

Typically, therapists encounter <u>anger</u>, <u>people who are depressed</u>, and <u>resentment.</u>

What makes that sentence non-parallel is that *not all* the list items are grammatically similar: *anger* and *resentment* are each nouns, but "people who are depressed" is a clause. Below are two ways to make all of the list items parallel.

EXAMPLES: **Parallel Structure**

1. Typically, therapists encounter <u>anger</u>, <u>depression</u>, and <u>resentment</u>.

2. Typically, therapists encounter <u>people who are angry</u>, <u>people who are depressed</u>, and <u>people who are resentful</u>.

<u>Sentence 1</u>: The list items are parallel because each list item is a noun.

<u>Sentence 2</u>: The list items are parallel because each list item is a clause.

Not all sentences lend themselves to parallel structure, especially if parts of the sentence address different types of concepts.

> **EXAMPLE: Sentence Not Well-Suited for Parallel Structure**
>
> The accident victim suffered a <u>concussion</u>, <u>pain</u>, and <u>he could not work for two months</u>.

Concussion and *pain* are nouns and are direct objects of *suffered*. The word *and* suggests that what follows is also a noun and direct object, but "he could not work for two months" is not a noun and cannot be a direct object (i.e., "he could not work for two months" is not something that one can suffer). One way to resolve the non-parallelism is to use two sentences.

> **EXAMPLE: Resolving Non-Parallel Structure by Using Two Sentences**
>
> The accident victim suffered a <u>concussion</u> and <u>pain</u>. He could not work for two months.

If you find yourself spending too much time struggling to make a sentence's list items parallel, consider addressing the material in two or more sentences.

B. A Court's Analysis of Parallel Structure

Beyond an issue of style or readability, parallelism can have an impact on a sentence's meaning—which is why courts have analyzed the parallel (or non-parallel) structure of text in legal documents.[8] The following is part of a California appellate-court judge's analysis of non-parallel language in a county ordinance:

Readers should pay particular attention to the **bungled parallelisms** in the first sentence:

No person shall <u>set up, use, operate</u> or <u>maintain</u> an <u>amplified sound system, music</u> and <u>live music</u> within any park, beach or recreational area except in those areas specifically designated, nor shall any person set up, use, operate or maintain an amplified sound system, music and live music without first obtaining a written permit.

Let us at the outset acknowledge that the **ordinance is poorly drafted**.... First, that "an" in front of "amplified sound system" thwarts the obvious and common sense parallelism which, judging from the overall nature of the ordinance, was intended by the drafter. In English grammar you don't say, "an music," "an live music," "an amplified music" or "an amplified live music," so you can't make the parallel series start after the "an" or the "an amplified."

Grammatically, the **parallel series must begin after "maintain."** But, so read, the series consists of, literally: (1) an amplified sound system; (2) music; and (3) live music. And if that's the series, the ordinance is clearly overbroad because, literally, it would require a permit to "maintain ... music" in the park. You would need a permit to hum a tune under that reading.

Of course, this raises the collateral question, how exactly does one "set up, use, operate or maintain ... music?" A singer might "maintain" a high C for a period of time, a rock band might "maintain a beat," but "maintain ... music" is **awkwardness bordering on unintelligibility.** [9] [Emphasis and paragraph breaks added.]

Parallel structure can require more words than non-parallel structure, but the benefits can outweigh the costs—especially in drafting legal documents.

VII. AVOIDING PROBLEMS WITH MODIFIERS

A. Placement of Modifiers

Modifiers should be placed so that it is clear to the reader which element of the sentence the modifier is describing, qualifying, or explaining—unless the writer intends to create ambiguity.

Modifiers such as *only* (which can be an adverb or an adjective) are tricky because (1) they can be correctly placed after or before the term that they modify and (2) they can correctly modify different types of terms (e.g., other modifiers, nouns, or verbs). Modifier placement can change a sentence's meaning.

EXAMPLES: **Moving *Only* Changes the Meaning**

1. <u>Only</u> she drank wine at the party.
2. She drank wine <u>only</u> at the party.
3. She drank wine at the party <u>only</u>.

<u>Sentence 1</u>: *Only* is isolated from everything but *she*, so *only* clearly modifies *she*. The meaning: she was the only person who drank wine at the party (e.g., everyone else drank soda or beer).

<u>Sentence 2</u>: *Only* is between *wine* and *at the party*. If *only* modifies *wine*, the meaning is that she drank nothing but wine. If *only* modifies *at the party*, then she drank the wine there but nowhere else (e.g., not in the car on the way home).

<u>Sentence 3</u>: *Only* is isolated from everything but *at the party*, meaning that she drank the wine nowhere else.

Because poor placement of a modifier can create ambiguity or confusion, we recommend that you make a habit of following the tips below.

> ### EXAMPLES: **Ways to Prevent or Solve Modifier-Placement Problems**
>
> 1. Place a modifier so that it can modify one term only, or
>
> 2. Rephrase a sentence to make clear which term a modifier is modifying.

Back to the she-drank-wine example, how would we clearly state that wine was the only drink that she drank? We could either (1) reorder more words than *only* or (2) completely rephrase the sentence.

> ### EXAMPLES: **Wine Was the Only Drink**
>
> • **Reordering**
> At the party, she drank <u>wine</u> only.
>
> • **Rephrasing**
> She drank nothing but <u>wine</u> at the party.
> <u>Wine</u> was the only thing that she drank at the party.

In some cases, a misplaced modifier might create momentary confusion, but context would enable the reader to figure out the intended meaning.

> ### EXAMPLE: **Ambiguity Resolved by Context**
>
> A car was reported stolen <u>by the police</u>.

The modifier *by the police* is placed where it can modify nothing but *stolen* (meaning that the police had stolen the car). The more likely intended meaning is that the police had reported the car stolen. There are at least two ways to rephrase the stolen-car sentence to convey that meaning without having to rely on context.

EXAMPLES: **Ambiguity Resolved through Rewriting**

1. The police reported that a car was stolen.
2. A car was reported by the Police to have been stolen.

Note for Lawyers: Some misplaced modifiers can cause serious ambiguity if nothing in the context resolves the question of intended meaning.

EXAMPLE: **Ambiguity <u>Not</u> Resolved by Context**

If the Buyer returns the goods, <u>no later than June 10</u>, the Seller will send a refund to Buyer.

Is June 10 the deadline for the Buyer's returning the goods or for the Seller's sending a refund? Below are examples of how to fix the sentence by moving the modifier so that it applies (1) to the Seller's sending of the refund and (2) to the Buyer's returning of the goods.

> EXAMPLES: **Ambiguity Resolved through Movement of Modifier**
>
> 1. If the Buyer returns the goods, the Seller will send a refund to the Buyer <u>no later than June 10</u>.
> 2. If the Buyer, <u>no later than June 10</u>, returns the goods, the Seller will send a refund to the Buyer.

<u>Sentence 1</u>: The ambiguity is resolved because the modifier is in a position where it can modify one thing only: *will send*.

<u>Sentence 2</u>: The modifier can logically modify *returns* but nothing else (the deadline cannot logically apply to the noun *Buyer*).

B. Phrasing of Modifiers

One of the most common problems caused by the mis-phrasing of a modifier is the **dangling modifier.** A dangling modifier does not attach grammatically (or otherwise) to the word or phrase that it is intended to describe, qualify, or explain.

> EXAMPLES: **Dangling Modifiers**
>
> 1. Erik's car collided with Claire's car <u>to avoid hitting a dog</u>.
> 2. <u>After considering the application</u>, the permit shall be issued.

♦ Dangling Modifier

Sentence 1: *To avoid hitting a dog* clearly modifies *Erik's car.* The literal meaning is nonsensical because Erik's car is not capable of having motive or intent. Obviously, *to avoid hitting a dog* is meant to modify *Erik* but cannot do so because *Erik* is not the subject of the sentence (*Erik's car* is the subject). The sentence's phrasing prevents the modifier from logically applying to anything that is actually in the sentence. Thus, the modifier is left "dangling."

Sentence 2: The sentence structure signals that "after considering the application" modifies the main clause's subject (*the permit*), but a permit is not capable of considering anything. Context suggests that some unnamed government office shall consider the application before issuing the permit, but that government office is absent from the sentence.

EXAMPLES: Dangling Modifiers Corrected

1. To avoid hitting a dog, Erik swerved, and his car collided with Claire's.
2. After considering the application, the Department shall issue the permit.

Unless you have a good reason for doing otherwise, we recommend that you carefully phrase modifiers so that (1) they are grammatically correct, (2) they make sense, and (3) it is obvious to which term the modifier applies.

C. Restrictive and Non-Restrictive Modifiers

A **restrictive modifier** is necessary to identify a particular person, place, or thing—to distinguish it from other persons, places, or things. **Note for Lawyers**: When analyzing legal text, courts have considered whether modifiers were restrictive or non-restrictive.[10]

EXAMPLES: **Restrictive Modifier**

1. The doctor examined the patient <u>who had a broken leg</u> before examining the other four patients.

2. Of all the cars that Brian had test-driven, he preferred the one <u>that had dual exhausts</u>.

<u>Sentence 1</u>: The modifier "who had a broken leg" is necessary to distinguish one patient from the other four patients (who did not have broken legs).

<u>Sentence 2</u>: The modifier "that had dual exhausts" is necessary to distinguish the car that Brian preferred from the other cars that Brian had test-driven.

A **non-restrictive modifier** is *not necessary* for identification: one could delete the modifier without changing the sentence's essential meaning because the non-restrictive modifier is merely additional information.

> EXAMPLES: **Non-Restrictive Modifier**
> **at End of Sentence**
> (modifier underlined)
>
> 1. Betty greeted her husband, <u>who was wearing a guilty smile</u>.
> 2. Don totaled his motorcycle, <u>which had been his only motorized vehicle</u>.

Sentence 1: The modifier "who was wearing a guilty smile" is not necessary to distinguish the husband from anyone else because Betty—at that time, anyway—had only one husband.

Sentence 2: The modifier "which was his only motorized vehicle" is not necessary to distinguish the motorcycle from any other motorcycle because Don had only one motorized vehicle.

Choosing between *that* **and** *which* relates to restrictive and non-restrictive modifiers. The traditional rules[11] are as follows:

(1) Use *that* and no commas to signify a restrictive modifier.

(2) Use *which* and at least one comma to signify a
    non-restrictive modifier.

> **EXAMPLE: Restrictive Modifier (*That*)**
>
> The gallery <u>that Linda opened</u> is located in New York City.

If we remove the restrictive modifier, the sentence would read "The gallery is located in New York City." The *that*-clause is necessary to distinguish one gallery (the one that Linda opened) from many others in New York City.

> **EXAMPLE: Non-Restrictive Modifier (*Which*)**
>
> New York City's Chrysler Building, <u>which is located on Lexington Avenue</u>, was completed in 1930.

The *which*-clause, which is enclosed within commas, tells us that the modifier is not essential to distinguish the building from any other building: New York City has only one Chrysler Building. The bit about Lexington Avenue is non-essential information.

Usage note: Some writers use *which* for both restrictive and non-restrictive modifiers[12] and rely on the presence or absence of commas to signify whether the *which*-modifier is restrictive or non-restrictive. We recommend that you follow the traditional rule if you are engaged in formal writing.

VIII. QUESTIONABLE TRADITIONS STATED AS "RULES"

A. Splitting Infinitives

An **infinitive** contains *to* + the base form of a verb (e.g., *to advise*). A **split infinitive** contains at least one word between the *to* and the verb (e.g., *to strongly advise*).

Although some people feel that splitting an infinitive is a grammatical sin, split infinitives **are not grammatically incorrect** according to authoritative sources ranging from at least the 1940s and into the new millennium.[13] Reportedly, the so-called rule against split infinitives emerged in the 1860s, when a British author opined that infinitives should not be split. Even before the twentieth century, the "rule" was somewhat controversial. For example, in a scathing letter to a newspaper editor in the 1890s, Irish writer George Bernard Shaw railed against the "rule."

In some cases, a writer might have stylistic reasons for splitting an infinitive. Consider the following snippet from the opening of the original *Star Trek* television series (an example used by many writers while explaining split infinitives).

EXAMPLES: **Split Infinitive (*Star Trek*)**

Original:
<u>To</u> **boldly** <u>go</u> where no man has gone before.

Two Other Options
1. **Boldly** <u>to go</u> where no man has gone before.
2. <u>To go</u> **boldly** where no man has gone before.

Options 1 and 2 have the same essential meaning as the original, but all three sound different because the emphasis on *boldly* is different. The best place for *boldly* depends on what sort of emphasis and sound the writer had intended to create.

While there is nothing wrong with splitting an infinitive to achieve a stylistic effect or avoid awkwardness, placing too many words between *to* and the verb can make a sentence hard to grasp. We recommend that you refrain from using more than a word or two (maybe three) to split an infinitive.

Warning: Reality aside, some readers might believe that a split infinitive violates a real rule—perhaps because they had been smacked with a ruler in grade school for splitting an infinitive. That said, splitting your infinitives might reduce your credibility, however undeservedly, in some readers' minds. Thus, you might refrain from splitting infinitives when writing for certain audiences.

B. Ending a Sentence with a Preposition

Some people object to ending a sentence with a preposition, though authoritative sources indicate that doing so is **not grammatically incorrect**.[14] For example, super-grammarian H.W. Fowler stated decades ago that the rule against ending a sentence with a preposition was rooted in superstition.[15] Usage expert Bryan Garner stated that the "rule" is nonsensical.[16] Style gurus Strunk and White stated that the end of a sentence is sometimes the best spot for a preposition.[17]

EXAMPLES: **Sentences Ending with a Preposition**

1. The client was difficult to reason <u>with</u>.
2. Whom did you give the book <u>to</u>?
3. Where is he <u>from</u>?

Back in the 1940s, acclaimed orator Winston Churchill reportedly stated the following to show his objection to the "rule" against ending a sentence with a preposition:

"This is the kind of tedious nonsense <u>up with which I will not put</u>!" [18]

Reportedly, when Churchill was the Prime Minister of England, a government clerk objected to the ending of a sentence with a preposition. Churchill mockingly responded by showing how awkward a sentence could sound (the underlined part) if a writer strained to avoid ending a sentence with a preposition.

Despite opposition from authoritative sources, some readers might *believe* that it is incorrect to end a sentence with a preposition. If you feel uncomfortable ending a sentence with a preposition, don't do it—just try to not create the sort of awkwardness that Mr. Churchill wryly pointed out.

IX. DEAL-BREAKING ERRORS

A. Grammar-Related Errors

Not all grammatical errors are created equal. There are some errors that even people who have not studied grammar will recognize. The following is a list of some deal-breaking errors (the errors are underlined).

- **Subject-Verb disagreement:**
  [e.g., The boy do not read.]

- **Verb-Tense error:**
  [e.g., He had gave it to me.]

- **Pronoun-case error:**
  [e.g., She had lunch with John and I.]

- **Pronoun-number error:**
  [e.g., A defendant should consult their lawyer.]

- **Sentence fragment:**
  [e.g., To quote the court of appeals.]

- **Comma splice:**
  [e.g., She ran, he walked.]

- **Apostrophe errors:**
  [e.g., her's or our's; misusing it's or its.]

B. Word-Choice-Related Errors

Misusing a word will prevent you from accurately conveying your intended meaning. Beware of words that sound like the words that you actually intend to use but that have different definitions. The following are examples of words that people commonly mix up and misuse:

- Accept and Except
- Allusion and Illusion
- Averse and Adverse
- Capitol and Capital
- Collaborate and Corroborate
- Complement and Compliment
- Disinterested and Uninterested
- Discreet and Discrete
- Eminent and Imminent
- Ensure and Insure

- Evoke and Invoke
- Inequity and Iniquity
- Judicial and Judicious
- Luxurious and Luxuriant
- Perspective and Prospective
- Precede and Proceed
- Prescribe and Proscribe
- Principal and Principle
- Reek and Wreak
- Stationary and Stationery

Do you know the difference between each word in each pair listed above? If not, look up any unfamiliar words in a dictionary.

Endnotes for Chapter 1 (Grammar)

1   *E.g.*, Amway Corp. v. Procter & Gamble Co., 346 F.3d 180, 187 (6th Cir. 2003) (citing *Harbrace* when discussing a coordinating conjunction in a statute); In re Hopkins, 371 B.R. 324, 326 (Bankr. N.D. Ill. 2007) (citing the *Harbrace* and *Prentice-Hall* grammar guides when discussing modifier placement in a statutory provision); American Family Mut. Ins. Co. v. Tickle, 99 S.W.3d 25, 30-31 (Mo. Ct. App. 2003) (citing *The Bedford Handbook* regarding a clause in an insurance policy); State v. Sosa, 223 P.3d 348, 352 (N.M. 2009) (citing *Harbrace* when analyzing a verb in a court transcript).

2   *E.g.*, Gonsalves v. City of W. Haven, 653 A.2d 156, 159 n.10 (Conn. 1995) (when discussing the use of a coordinating conjunction in legislation, the court cites two grammar handbooks: P. Roberts's *Understanding Grammar* and *The Harbrace College Handbook*); Eagle Leasing Corp. v. Hartford Fire Ins. Co., 384 F. Supp. 247, 251 n.1 (E.D. Tex. 1974) (when discussing modifier placement in the context of an insurance policy, the court cites four grammar handbooks: *The Harbrace College Handbook*, Fowler's *Modern English Usage*, Strunk and White's *The Elements of Style*, and Walsh's *Plain English Handbook*); AIU Ins. Co. v. Robert Plan Corp., 2006 WL 3904521, *2-3 (N.Y. Sup., 2006) (when discussing restrictive versus non-restrictive modifiers in the context of an agreement, the court cites three grammar-related books: Strunk and White's *The Elements of Style*, Fowler's *A Dictionary of Modern English Usage*, and *The New Fowler's Modern English Usage*).

3   *E.g.*, Allard K. Lowenstein Int'l Human Rights Project v. Dep't of Homeland Sec., 626 F.3d 678, 581 (2d Cir. 2010) (court used the term *modifier*); Regents of University of Minnesota v. AGA Medical Corp, No. 07-CV-4732, 2011 WL 6256984, *15 (D. Minn. Dec. 14, 2011) (court used the term *prepositional phrase*); Mid-Century Ins. Co. v. Robles, 271 P.3d 592, 595-96 (Colo. Ct. App. 2011) (court used the term *independent clause*); In re Arnott, 942 N.E.2d 1124, 1135, (Ohio Ct. App. 2010) (court used the term *dependent clause*); Leza v. State, 351 S.W.3d 344, 356-57 (Tex. Crim. App. 2011) (court used the term *direct object*).

4   *E.g.*, CHERYL GLENN AND LORETTA GRAY, THE HODGES HARBRACE HANDBOOK 101 (18th ed., Wadsworth, 2012) (listing the progressive "tense" in a table of verb tenses); DIANA HACKER, THE BEDFORD HANDBOOK: INSTRUCTOR'S ANNOTATED EDITION 378-79 (5th ed. 1998) (labeling the progressive as a "form").

♦ Endnotes

5   *E.g.*, Campbell v. Dist. of Columbia, 568 A.2d 1076, 1078 (D.C.1990); Kar v. Nanda, 805 N.W.2d 609, 612 (Mich. Ct. App. 2011); TAC Associates v. New Jersey Dep't of Envtl. Prot., 998 A.2d 450, 456-57 (N.J. 2010).

6   *E.g.*, Vaden v. Discover Bank, 556 U.S. 49, 76 (2009) (discussing the subjunctive mood); United States v. Weingarten, 632 F.3d 60, 65-66 (2d Cir. 2011) (discussing the subjunctive mood); United States v. Reth, 364 Fed. App'x 323, 325 (9th Cir. 2010) (discussing the subjunctive mood).

7   *See e.g.*, CHERYL GLENN AND LORETTA GRAY, THE HODGES HARBRACE HANDBOOK 105-06, (18th ed., Wadsworth, 2012); BRYAN A. GARNER, THE REDBOOK: A MANUAL ON LEGAL STYLE 144-45 (2002); JOHN E. WARRINER, ENGLISH GRAMMAR AND COMPOSITION 157-58 (Franklin Ed., Harcourt Brace Jovanovich, 1982).

8   *E.g.*, U.S. ex rel. Totten v. Bombardier Corp., 380 F.3d 488, 499-500 (D.C. Cir. 2004); Fluor Enterprises, Inc. v. Revenue Div., Dep't of Treasury, 730 N.W.2d 722, 732 n.3 (Mich. 2007); City of Portland By & Through Portland Dev. Comm'n v. Smith, 838 P.2d 568, 577 (Or. 1992) (Graber, J., dissenting).

9   Shariat v. County of Orange, No. G034807, 2006 WL 1660576, *1-2 (Cal. Ct. App. June 16, 2006).

10   *E.g.*, Janvey v. Democratic Senatorial Campaign Comm., 793 F. Supp. 2d 825, 839 (N.D. Tex. 2011) (considering the effect of a restrictive modifier when analyzing a statute); Benson v. City of Birmingham, 659 So. 2d 82, 85 (Ala. 1995) (considering a non-restrictive modifier when analyzing a statute); Meamber v. Oregon Pac. Bank, Inc., 239 Or. App. 479, 482-83 (2010) (considering the effect of a restrictive modifier when analyzing a trust deed).

11   *That* is still correct for restrictive modifiers but not for non-restrictive modifiers. However, there seems to be some wiggle room regarding *which*: some writers use *which* in either a restrictive or non-restrictive modifier, and the comma (or its absence) determines whether the modifier is restrictive or non-restrictive. *See e.g.*, CHERYL GLENN & LORETTA GRAY, THE HODGES HARBRACE HANDBOOK 73-74 (18th ed., Wadsworth, 2012); WILLIAM STRUNK & E.B. WHITE, THE ELEMENTS OF STYLE 59 (50th Anniversary ed., Pearson Longman, 2009); DIANA HACKER, THE BEDFORD HANDBOOK 434 (5th ed. 1998).

12   *E.g.*, CHERYL GLENN AND LORETTA GRAY, THE HODGES HARBRACE HANDBOOK, 74 (18th ed., Wadsworth, 2012) (explaining that some professional writers use *which* for either a restrictive or non-restrictive modifier); DIANA HACKER, THE BEDFORD HANDBOOK: INSTRUCTOR'S ANNOTATED EDITION 434 (5th ed. 1998) (stating that usage varies in terms of whether to use *which* for either a restrictive or non-restrictive modifier); H. RAMSEY FOWLER, THE LITTLE, BROWN HANDBOOK 561 (2d. ed., 1983) (stating that *which* can be used to introduce both restrictive and non-restrictive modifiers).

13   *E.g.*, JOHN C. HODGES, HARBRACE HANDBOOK OF ENGLISH 279 (1ˢᵗ ed. 1941) (advising the reader to avoid splitting an infinitive *if* awkwardness results); H. W. FOWLER, A DICTIONARY OF MODERN ENGLISH USAGE 581 (edited by Sir Ernest Gowers, 2d ed., Oxford University Press, 1965) (stating that splitting an infinitive is preferable to creating ambiguity or artificiality); BRYAN A. GARNER, THE REDBOOK: A MANUAL ON LEGAL STYLE 151 (2002) (advising the reader to split the infinitive if the reader wants to achieve certain effects but to avoid splitting the infinitive if the reader is uncomfortable with doing so); DIANA HACKER, THE BEDFORD HANDBOOK: INSTRUCTOR'S ANNOTATED EDITION 217 (5th ed. 1998) (stating that it is acceptable to split the infinitive to avoid an unnatural-sounding construction); LAURA G. KIRSZNER AND STEPHEN R. MANDELL, THE HOLT HANDBOOK 439 (6th ed. 2002) (stating that splitting the infinitive is acceptable if the modifier is not long); GORDON LOBERGER AND KATE SHOUP, WEBSTER'S NEW WORLD ENGLISH GRAMMAR HANDBOOK 204-05 (2d ed. 2009) (stating that a split infinitive can sound better than an un-split infinitive and that avoiding splitting an infinitive can create an awkward-sounding construction); WILLIAM STRUNK, JR. AND E.B. WHITE, THE ELEMENTS OF STYLE 78 (50th Anniversary ed., Pearson Longman, 2009) (advising the reader to split the infinitive if the result is clear and sounds better than leaving the infinitive un-split—the same advice that Strunk and White gave in the book's third edition, published in 1979).

14   *E.g.*, JOHN C. HODGES, HARBRACE COLLEGE HANDBOOK 12-13 (4th ed. 1956) (stating that in some cases a sentence is more natural sounding if the preposition is at the end); H. W. FOWLER, A DICTIONARY OF MODERN ENGLISH USAGE 473-75 (edited by Sir Ernest Gowers, 2d ed., Oxford University Press, 1965) (advising that the reader not blindly follow the traditional prohibition on ending a sentence with a preposition); WILLIAM STRUNK, JR. AND E.B. WHITE, THE ELEMENTS OF STYLE 77-78 (3d. ed., MacMillan, 1979) (stating that it is acceptable, and sometimes preferable, to end a sentence with a preposition—a statement that Strunk and White repeated in the book's fiftieth anniversary edition, published in 2009); BRYAN A. GARNER, THE REDBOOK: A MANUAL ON LEGAL STYLE 123 (2002) (stating that the prohibition against ending a sentence with a preposition is nonsensical).

15   H. W. FOWLER, A DICTIONARY OF MODERN ENGLISH USAGE 473-75 (edited by Sir Ernest Gowers, 2d ed., Oxford University Press, 1965).

16   BRYAN A. GARNER, THE REDBOOK: A MANUAL ON LEGAL STYLE 123 (2002).

17   WILLIAM STRUNK, JR. AND E.B. WHITE, THE ELEMENTS OF STYLE 77-78 (50th Anniversary ed., Pearson Longman, 2009).

18   Different sources quote the first part of the sentence differently or describe the context differently, but they agree on Churchill's intended message. The Churchill Centre and Museum at the Churchill War Rooms, London, *Famous Quotations and Stories*, https://www.winstonchurchill.org/learn/speeches/quotations (last visited December 3, 2012) (citing the *New York Times* and *Chicago Tribune* and acknowledging that some sources quote the sentence as "This is the kind of tedious nonsense . . . , and others quote it as "This is the kind of pedantic nonsense . . ."); Washington State University, *Churchill on Prepositions*, http://public.wsu.edu/~brians/errors/churchill.html (last visited December 3, 2012) (citing *The American Heritage Book of English Usage* and stating (1) that the sentence was "This is the sort of English up with which I will not put" and (2) that the sentence was Churchill's response to an editor who had awkwardly rearranged Churchill's words to avoid splitting an infinitive).

CHAPTER 2.
Some Basics About Punctuation

I. THE IMPORTANCE OF PUNCTUATION

INCORRECT PUNCTUATION can affect the meaning of text, cause ambiguity, and make a writer seem poorly educated. **Note for Lawyers**: Courts have considered punctuation when construing legal documents.[1]

II. PERIODS

A. Period Ending a Sentence

In formal writing, use a period to end a *complete* sentence (as opposed to a sentence fragment).

> EXAMPLES: **Period at End of Sentence**
>
> • Wayne went to the store, and he bought wine.
> • Bill and Sean are hiking.

Do not put a period after a sentence fragment unless you are (1) writing informally (e.g., texting a friend); (2) quoting someone who used a sentence fragment; or (3) writing dialogue for a character who does not speak in complete sentences.

EXAMPLES: **Sentence Fragments**

- Went to work
  [*the verb's subject is missing*]

- A rebel without a cause
  [*the verb is missing*]

B. Period in Some Abbreviations

Some abbreviations contain at least one period.

EXAMPLES: **Period in Abbreviations**

• Dr. Baldwin	• 9:00 a.m.
• Mrs. Morris	• 5:00 p.m.
• John Adams, Jr.	• Smith vs. Jones

Consult a good dictionary regarding whether an abbreviation should contain a period. Also, check any style guide that is relevant to your type of writing, such as the *AP Style Guide* or *MLA Handbook*.

If an abbreviation takes a period and ends a sentence, use only one period at the end of the sentence.

EXAMPLES: **Abbreviation at End of Sentence**

- Joel left work at 6:00 p.m.
- Phyllis was listening to Hank Williams, Jr.

III. COMMAS

A. The Comma's Impact on Meaning

The comma is often misunderstood. Some people place a comma wherever they feel that readers should pause. Others place or omit a comma based on what they recall having been taught years earlier. One result is willy-nilly punctuation use that can cause confusion or ambiguity.

Because comma placement can affect the meaning of a sentence, we recommend that you use commas carefully and according to the rules. Consider the following examples.

◆ Commas

EXAMPLES: **Comma's Effect on Meaning**

1(a) Let's eat, Rodney.

1(b) Let's eat Rodney.

2(a) When the car struck, Bill James yelled.

2(b) When the car struck Bill, James yelled.

Sentence 1(a): The comma indicates that someone is speaking to Rodney, urging him to eat.

Sentence 1(b): Without the comma, *Rodney* is the direct object of *eat*: i.e., someone is suggesting that Rodney would be a tasty meal.

Sentence 2(a): One person is mentioned in the sentence (Bill James), and he yelled.

Sentence 2(b): Two people are mentioned (Bill and James); James is the one who yelled, and Bill was hit by the car.

Note for Lawyers: A Florida appellate court found a key provision in an insurance policy ambiguous, partly due to the "plethora of commas."[2] Similarly, a comma in a building-construction contract led to litigation that went all the way up to the South Carolina Supreme Court.[3]

B. Some Basic Comma-Usage Rules

1. Commas and Introductory Elements

Traditionally, a comma follows an introductory element that begins a sentence. Some writers omit the comma after the introductory element if it is short and if confusion would not result. We recommend the cautious approach: that you insert a comma after an introductory element.

EXAMPLES: **Introductory Elements**

- On May 28, Katie will fly to Madrid.
- After leaving work, Tracy went to the gym.
- If the Tenant fails to timely pay rent, the Tenant shall pay the Landlord a late fee.

---

2. Commas in a Series

Use commas to separate items in a series unless at least one of the items contains a comma; in that case, use semicolons (as discussed in Section IV). A **series** contains three or more items.

EXAMPLES: **Commas in a Series**

- John bought a book, a CD, and a DVD.
- The farmer harvested, packaged, and delivered the crop.

In the examples above, the comma that directly precedes each *and* is an *Oxford Comma* (also called a *Harvard Comma*). Some writers habitually insert the Oxford Comma before the conjunction. Some writers omit the Oxford Comma if its absence does not cause confusion. Whether you omit or insert the Oxford Comma is largely a judgment call.

3. Commas and Conjunctions

Use a comma before a coordinating conjunction that links two independent clauses (clauses that can stand alone as sentences). Conjunctions include words such as *and, but, or, nor,* and *yet.*

EXAMPLES: **Comma + Conjunction**
Separating Independent Clauses
(independent clauses underlined)

- <u>Tim played football,</u> and <u>his mother watched him.</u>
- <u>The dog barked,</u> yet the cat did not run.
- <u>The school's administrators were paid well,</u> but the teachers were not.

Don't place a comma before a conjunction that separates a sentence's subject from one of its two verbs.[4]

EXAMPLES: **No Comma Between**
Subject and One of Its Two Verbs
(verbs underlined)

- Jodi <u>wrote</u> a brief and <u>read</u> a stack of files.
- Neil <u>was</u> on vacation but <u>continued</u> to work.

If a subject has three or more verbs (i.e., a series of verbs), use commas and a conjunction to separate the verbs—the same way that you would use commas and a conjunction to separate a series of nouns, adjectives, or phrases.

♦ Commas in a Series of Verbs

EXAMPLES: **Commas in a Series of Verbs**
(verbs underlined)

- Bob <u>bought</u>, <u>packaged</u>, and <u>delivered</u> a gift.
- Jon <u>conducted</u> research, <u>wrote</u> a brief, and <u>filed</u> it with the court.

It is incorrect to separate two independent clauses by using a comma without a conjunction. That usage results in a comma splice, which is listed in Chapter 1 as a deal-breaking grammatical error.

EXAMPLE: **Comma Splice**

Gustavo sailed the boat, John enjoyed the ride.

EXAMPLES: **Ways to Fix the Comma Splice**

- Gustavo sailed the boat; John enjoyed the ride.
- Gustavo sailed the boat, **and** John enjoyed the ride.
- Gustavo sailed the boat. John enjoyed the ride.

---

4. Commas and Restrictive Versus Non-Restrictive Modifiers

Do not use any commas to set off a restrictive modifier from the rest of the sentence. Restrictive modifiers are necessary to distinguish what they are modifying from other people, places, or things (as discussed in Chapter 1, Section VII).

EXAMPLES: **Restrictive Modifiers (No Commas)**

- At the party, Janice avoided the man <u>who was speaking more loudly than anyone else</u>.
- Of the two articles that were due, the writer chose to work on the one <u>that was due earlier</u>.

Non-restrictive modifiers provide extra information and are not necessary to distinguish what they modify from other people, places, or things (as discussed in Chapter 1, Section VII).

If a non-restrictive modifier is at the end of a sentence, use a comma to set off the modifier from the rest of the sentence.

◆ Non-Restrictive & Restrictive Modifiers

EXAMPLES:
Non-Restrictive Modifier at End of Sentence
(modifier underlined)

- Betty greeted her husband, <u>who was wearing a guilty smile</u>.
- Don totaled his car, <u>which had been his only motorized vehicle</u>.

If a non-restrictive modifier is not at the end of a sentence, enclose the modifier within a pair of commas. For a restrictive modifier in a similar position, omit the commas.

EXAMPLES: **Modifiers Not at End of Sentence**
(modifier underlined)

1. Non-Restrictive (Commas)

The reporter, <u>who had never tried skydiving</u>, jumped out of the airplane.

2. Restrictive (No commas)

The reporter <u>who had never tried skydiving</u> jumped out of the airplane first; the other reporter jumped last.

Another option is to replace the comma or commas with a dash or pair of dashes. Dashes are discussed in Section VII.

IV. SEMICOLONS

A. Semicolons in a Series

Use semicolons to separate items in a series if at least one item contains a comma. If none of the items contains a comma, separate the items with commas (as illustrated in Section III.B.2).

EXAMPLES: **Semicolons Versus Commas in a Series**

1. Heidi met interesting people on the cruise: Dennis; Annie, a teacher; and Korinn.

2. Heidi met interesting people on the cruise: Dennis, Annie, a teacher, and Korinn.

Sentence 1: Heidi met **three people** (Dennis, Annie, and Korinn). The semicolons separate each item from the others. One item ("Annie, a teacher") contains descriptive information about Annie, which is set off by a comma.

Sentence 2: Heidi met **four people**: three are named, and one is not (Dennis, Annie, a teacher, and Korinn).

B. Semicolons and Independent Clauses

You could use a semicolon between related independent clauses (clauses that could stand alone as separate sentences) if the clauses are not linked by a coordinating conjunction. Another option is to use a colon, as discussed in Section V. If you use a semicolon between two independent clauses, don't include a coordinating conjunction.

EXAMPLES: **Semicolon Joining Independent Clauses**

- Rocky asked for a smart phone; Carl gave it to him.
- Inger wanted to go to Paris; her husband wanted to go to on a fishing trip.

If you prefer to separate two independent clauses with a coordinating conjunction, use a comma instead of a semicolon (as discussed in Section III.B.3).

V. COLONS

A. Colon and Independent Clauses

A colon signifies that something relevant is coming. You could use a colon to separate two independent clauses that are related.

EXAMPLES: **Colon Separating Independent Clauses**

- Dan found an interesting way to announce his presence at the party: he tumbled down the stairs.

- Kelsey did not understand why people called her brother "Curly": his hair was perfectly straight.

Another option is to use a semicolon (as discussed in Section IV.B).

B. Colon and a Series, Quote, or Explanation

Use a colon to introduce a series of items, a quote, or an explanation. The traditional rule is that an **independent clause** should precede the colon that is introducing a series, quote, or explanation.[5] What follows a colon *does not have to be* an independent clause.

♦ Colons

EXAMPLES: **Series, Quote, or Explanation**
(pre-colon independent clauses underlined)

1. <u>Three desserts were on the menu</u>: chocolate mousse, pecan pie, and lemon cake.

2. <u>The CEO said the following</u>: "My paycheck is huge because I want it that way."

3. <u>Lynn is an expert in bankruptcy law</u>: he has written many articles about the topic.

Many writers violate the traditional rule by not placing an independent clause before the colon.

EXAMPLES: **Violations of Traditional Rule**
(no independent clause before colon)

• The three available desserts were: cake, pie, and cookies.

• The CEO said: "Shareholders be damned, I want the money."

Though violations of the colon-and-independent-clause rule have become common, we recommend that you follow the traditional rule.

C. Colon after a Tag

It is common to place a colon after a word or phrase that acts as a tag (i.e., that labels the independent clause following the colon). Some handbooks do not address usage of a colon with a tag.[6]

EXAMPLES: **Tag Before a Colon**

• Usage note: The pronoun *they* should be used to refer to only a plural noun or noun substitute.

• Error alert: The pronoun *they* should not be used to refer to a singular noun.

D. Whether to Capitalize after Colon

Different sources say different things about whether to capitalize the first letter of the first word after a colon. For example, *The Chicago Manual of Style* states, in part, that the first word after a colon is not capitalized unless the word is a proper name or unless the colon introduces a quote or multiple sentences.[7] *The Bedford Handbook* and *The Redbook* state that the first letter of the first word in an independent clause that follows a colon could be either lower case or capitalized.[8]

Regarding a direct quote that follows a colon, most sources agree that the first word of the quote should be capitalized.

Regarding the use of a colon after a tag to call attention to words, one author prefers to capitalize the first word after the colon. The other author has no preference. Whichever way you choose, the key is to be consistent.

E. Spacing After a Colon

Different sources say different things about whether to insert one space or two spaces after a colon. According to *The Chicago Manual of Style*, for example, only one space should follow the colon.[9] The examples of colon usage in Strunk and White's *The Elements of Style* seem to include only one space after each colon, but the book does not state a preference.[10]

That said, many writers insert two spaces after a colon. Whether you insert one space or two spaces, the key is to be consistent.

VI. APOSTROPHES

A. Apostrophe Showing Possession

Use an apostrophe to show possession on the part of a noun. For a singular noun that does not end in *s*, add an apostrophe + *s*.

> EXAMPLES: **Singular Nouns Not Ending in S**
>
> • The girl**'s** computer   (one girl)
> • The boy**'s** clothing   (one boy)

For a singular noun that ends in *s*, you have a choice—though some style guides advocate using one way over the other.

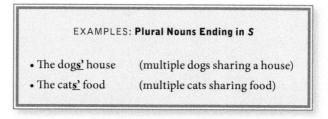

If a plural noun ends in *s*, add only an apostrophe.

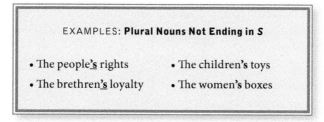

If a plural noun does not end in *s*, add an apostrophe + *s*.

EXAMPLES: **Plural Nouns Not Ending in S**

- The people's rights   • The children's toys
- The brethren's loyalty   • The women's boxes

If a family name ends in *s* or *z*, forming the plural possessive requires two steps: (1) pluralize the name by adding *es* and (2) add an apostrophe + *s*.

EXAMPLES: **Family Names Ending in S or Z**

- The Reynolds**es's** house
- The Martinez**es's** cat

To show joint possession, put the apostrophe after only the last noun. To show individual possession, put an apostrophe after each noun.

EXAMPLES: **Joint Versus Individual Possession**

Joint: Dan and Cindy**'s** house

Individual: Brenda**'s** and Jack**'s** cars

Dan and Cindy co-own one house (at least until the divorce is final). Brenda and Jack each have at least one car.

B. Apostrophe and Plurals of Numerals, Letters, and Words

Some writers use an apostrophe to form the plural of a numeral, a letter referred to as a letter, and a word referred to as word.

EXAMPLES: **Numeral, Letter, and Word**

- The phone number included two **5's**.
- The student earned three **A's** last semester.
- The song lyrics contained twenty *love's*.

C. Apostrophe in Contractions and Abbreviations

Use an apostrophe to show that a word is a contraction. A contraction is a shortened version of a word or word group and is created through the omission of at least one letter or syllable. The apostrophe signals that something was omitted.

EXAMPLES: **Common Contractions**

- Don't   (a contraction of *do not*).
- Would've   (a contraction of *would have*).
- It's   (a contraction of *it is*).

♦ Apostrophes

★ **Common-Error Alert:** The unintended absence or presence of an apostrophe can result in a word that you did not intend to use and that spell check probably would not flag. Consider the following examples:

- Won't   (a contraction of *will not*)
- Wont   (an adjective meaning *accustomed*)

Contractions can make text sound more natural and flowing, but some readers object to the contraction's informality. **Note for Lawyers:** We recommend that you avoid contractions when writing legal text.

Apostrophes are also used in some abbreviations to show the omission of at least one letter or number: e.g., *Gov't* (meaning *government*) or the *'80s* (meaning the *1980s*).

VII. DASHES

A. Typing the Dash

To form a dash (an *em dash*), type two hyphens (--), and leave no space between the dash and the word on either side of the dash. Some word-processing programs automatically change the two hyphens into a single dash. If your program does not do so, then use two hyphens.

B. Creating Emphasis with Dashes

To set off words that you want to emphasize, use a single dash or a pair of dashes. If the emphasized words are at the end of the sentence, use a single dash.

EXAMPLES: **Single Dash**

- Black and white—those were the only colors that the party guests wore.
- The Defendant broke several laws—the least significant being trespassing.

If the emphasized words are not at the beginning or end of the sentence, use a pair of dashes.

EXAMPLES: **Pair of Dashes**

- Carol's two favorite painters—Renoir and Cassatt—were impressionists.
- Greg had to work late on most nights—though his wife preferred otherwise—because his job was demanding.

Another option is to use a comma or pair of commas to set off words in a sentence (as discussed in Section III.B.4), but the emphasis would be different.

C. Dashes and a Series of Words

Sometimes a dash is necessary to isolate a series of modifying words within a main clause. If the sentence already contains one or more commas, embedding such a series between a pair of commas won't work well.

EXAMPLES: **Pair of Dashes Versus Commas**

• **Clear (dashes)**
Only three of the menu items—pizza, burgers, and wings—appealed to Louis.

• **Confusing (commas)**
Only three of the menu items, pizza, burgers, and wings, appealed to Louis.

Another option is to use parentheses instead of a pair of dashes, but some readers might perceive the parentheses as signaling that the language is of secondary importance.

D. Dash Introducing a List

A writer could use a dash to introduce a list.

EXAMPLE: **Introducing a List**

The Defendant was guilty of three counts—armed robbery, trafficking in stolen goods, and speeding.

Another option is to introduce the list with a colon and an independent clause, as discussed in Section V.B.

VIII. HYPHENS

A. Typing the Hyphen

A hyphen requires a single stroke of the hyphen key (-). Do not insert a blank space before or after a hyphen.

B. Hyphen with Prefixes and Compound Words

When attached to a word, some prefixes must be followed by a hyphen. Similarly, some compound words require a hyphen between the words.

> EXAMPLES: **Prefix and Compound Word**
>
> • Richard and his <u>ex-wife</u> had lunch together.
> • The attorney <u>cross-examined</u> the witness.

There is no simple rule for determining whether a prefix or compound word requires hyphenation. You would have to consult a dictionary.

C. Hyphen with Compound Adjective

A compound adjective is two or more words that function together as one adjective. If a compound adjective comes **before** the noun that it modifies, use a hyphen (or hyphens) to join the words that form the compound adjective.

EXAMPLES: **Compound Adjectives**

1(a) Bonnie has a <u>sky-blue</u> **car.**   (hyphen)

1(b) Bonnie's **car** is sky blue.   (no hyphen)

2(a) A <u>well-written</u> **novel** is enjoyable.   (hyphen)

2(b) Grisham's **novels** are well written.   (no hyphen)

Don't place a hyphen between an adverb that ends in -*ly* and the adjective that the adverb modifies.

EXAMPLES: **No Hyphen between *ly*-Adverb and Adjective**

- **Correct:**   Merrill's intensly blue eyes flashed.
- Incorrect: Merrill's intensely-blue eyes flashed.

IX. QUESTION MARKS

Use a question mark at the end of a direct question, whether the question is an entire sentence or is only part of a sentence.

EXAMPLES: **Direct Questions**

- Susan asked Rick, "Do you want a drink?"
- What did Rick drink?

Put a period (not a question mark) at the end of an indirect question.

EXAMPLES: **Indirect Questions**

- Peg asked Ron to go to lunch.
- Larry asked whether the motion had been filed.

X. QUOTATION MARKS

A. Quotes that Are Block-Indented

Block-indented quotes are generally *not* enclosed by quotation marks: the indentation signifies that the block of material is being directly quoted. If a block quote contains material that is quoted from another source, then use double quotation marks for the quote within the quote.

EXAMPLE: **Block Quote**

The candidate said the following:

One of history's most successful political propagandists once said, "If you tell a lie big enough and keep repeating it, people will eventually come to believe it." That man worked for Adolf Hitler.

Style guides differ regarding whether a quote has to be of a certain length to be block-indented. For example, *The Bluebook* (a guide for legal writers) recommends block-indented format for quotes that contain at least 50 words.[11] Some style guides do not mention a minimum length and contain examples of block quotes that contain fewer than 50 words.

B. Quotes that are Not Block-Indented

If a quote is within a paragraph and not block-indented, use double quotation marks to set off (1) direct quotes of writing or speech and (2) thoughts that resemble speech.

EXAMPLES: **Double Quotation Marks**

- **Direct Quote** (Speech or Writing)
  When receiving the award, the novelist said,
  "I am grateful to my readers."

- **Thought Resembling Speech**
  "When dogs fly," I thought, as I looked at the car's
  sticker price.

Unless the larger body of quoted material is block-indented, use single quotation marks to signify a quote within a quote.

EXAMPLE: **Single Quotation Marks**

The speaker said the following: "The Declaration
of Independence states that all people 'are created
equal,' and I'm quoting that document directly."

In the previous example, everything within the double quotation marks is what the speaker said. The single quotation marks around the underlined clause indicate that the speaker was quoting the words of someone else.

If material is paraphrased, don't use quotation marks. Paraphrased material is often preceded by *that*.

EXAMPLES: **Quoted and Paraphrased Material**

- **Quoted**
  Pam said, "I wanted a martini."

- **Paraphrased**
  Pam said that she wanted a martini.

C. Quotes and Words Referred to as Words

You could use quotation marks to indicate that a word is being referred to as a word. It seems to be a matter of choice: some handbooks suggest using quotation marks, some suggest using italics, and some state that either choice would work.[12] The key is to be consistent.

> **EXAMPLES: Word Referred to as a Word**
>
> • The word "love" is often used to label what actually amounts to infatuation.
> • The word *love* is often used to label what actually amounts to infatuation.

D. Quotes and Titles of Some Works

Use quotes to indicate the title of a short work, such as an essay, short story, magazine article, poem, or song. [13] For longer works—such as books, films, plays, and magazines—italicize the title. [14]

> **EXAMPLES: Quoting Versus Italicizing Title**
>
> • *The Triangle* is a book that Carol edited.
> • "The Cask of Amontillado" is a short story written by Edgar Allen Poe.

E. Punctuating Quoted Language

1. Periods and Commas with Quotes

The rule in the U.S. is that a period or comma at the end of a quote goes **inside** the final quotation mark.[15]

EXAMPLES: **Period and Comma with Quotes**

- "Just make money—I don't want to know how you do it," the CEO said.
- The CEO said, "Just make money—I don't want to know how you do it."

---

2. Colons and Semicolons with Quotes

The rule in the U.S. is that a colon or semicolon at the end of a quote goes **outside** the final quotation mark.[16]

EXAMPLES: **Colon and Semicolon with Quotes**

- The poet repeatedly used two words in the poem "The Psychotic State of Loving": *love* and *hate*.
- The landlord wrote to the tenant "Your rent is two weeks late"; the tenant did not respond.

---

3. Question Marks with Quotes

Place a question mark **inside** the quotation marks if the quote is the question; place the question mark **outside** the quotation marks if the entire sentence is the question but the quoted material is not.[17]

EXAMPLES: **Question Marks and Quotes**

• Quoted material is the question
  Scott asked, "Should we eat out tonight?"

• Entire sentence is a question but the quote *is not*
  When did Michelle say "I want a divorce"?

XI. ELLIPSES

A. Ellipsis Points and Material Omitted from a Quote

1. Description of Ellipsis Points

A set of **ellipsis points** (also called an *ellipsis mark*) contains three dots and might precede or follow another punctuation mark. Ellipsis points indicate the omission of material. **Note:** *Ellipses* (with a second *e*) refers to more than one set of ellipsis points, not to a single set.

2. Typing of Ellipsis Points

To form ellipsis points, type three periods (. . .), and insert a space between each period. If a period precedes or follows ellipsis points, type four periods (. . . .), and insert a space between each period.

3. Omission of Partial or Full Sentences

Use ellipsis points to indicate the omission from quoted material of at least a partial sentence or full sentence. There are multiple methods for using ellipsis points. For example, *The Chicago Manual of Style* sets out three distinct methods.[18] *The Bluebook,* which is for legal writers, recommends a method that shares characteristics of some other methods yet differs in some ways.

We recommend that you use the method described in this section unless you need to follow a different convention (e.g., a journalist might follow *The Associated Press Stylebook*).

Use **three dots** (the ellipsis points) to indicate the omission of at least one word from a quoted sentence unless the omitted material begins the quoted sentence. Many sources agree that ellipsis points *should not* be used to indicate omission of the beginning of a quoted sentence.[19]

EXAMPLE: **Full-Sentence Quote**

Dr. Siler said, "I analyzed 12 so-called *air fresheners,* and each one emitted chemicals—such as benzene, formaldehyde, or phthalates—that are toxic."

> ### EXAMPLE: **Partial Quote with Ellipsis Points**
>
> After analyzing 12 air fresheners, Dr. Siler said, "each one emitted chemicals . . . that are toxic."

The ellipsis points indicate the omission of part of Dr. Siler's sentence ("such as benzene, formaldehyde, or phthalates" and the two dashes). Notice that the beginning of Dr. Siler's sentence was omitted from the partial quote, yet the partial quote does not begin with ellipsis points.

Use **four dots** (a period plus the ellipsis points) to indicate either of the following:

(1) that your sentence ends with a partial quote, or

(2) that you omitted at least one sentence from a multi-sentence quote.

> ### EXAMPLE: **Full, Multi-Sentence Quote**
>
> Dr. Siler said, "I analyzed 12 so-called air fresheners, and each one emitted chemicals—such as benzene, formaldehyde, or phthalates—that are toxic. Some of those chemicals can cause lung damage or brain damage or birth defects. Yet, those products are advertised on TV."

♦ Ellipses

EXAMPLE: **Ending Your Sentence with a Partial Quote**

Dr. Siler analyzed 12 air fresheners and said, "Some of those chemicals can cause lung damage or brain damage. . . ."

EXAMPLE: **Omission of at Least One Sentence from Multi-Sentence Quote**

Dr. Siler said, "I analyzed 12 so-called *air fresheners*, and each one emitted chemicals—such as benzene, formaldehyde, or phthalates—that are toxic. . . . Yet, those products are advertised on TV."

Note for Lawyers: *The Bluebook's* method for using ellipsis points differs somewhat from the method that we discuss. We recommend that you use *The Bluebook's* method when engaged in legal writing for an audience that expects writers to follow *The Bluebook*.

4. Omission of Full and Partial Paragraphs

There are multiple methods for indicating that at least one full paragraph was omitted from a multi-paragraph quote.[20] Seeking to simplify matters, we recommend that you use the method discussed in this subsection unless you need to follow a different convention.

If you omit at least one full paragraph from a multi-paragraph quote, put four dots at the end of the paragraph that precedes any omitted paragraphs.

EXAMPLE: **Omitted Full Paragraph**
Followed by Full Paragraph

The teacher explained the following to his sixth-grade class:

The Constitution gives us rights. For example, we have the right to say what we want and to choose our friends. . . .

Rights are great, but that our rights are listed on paper means nothing. For our rights to truly matter, we must exercise and protect them.

The four dots at the end of the first paragraph indicate the omission of at least one entire paragraph from the quote.

If you omit material from the beginning of the quoted paragraph that directly follows the four dots, place three dots at the beginning of the partially quoted paragraph.

EXAMPLE: Omitted Full Paragraph Followed by Partially Quoted Paragraph

The teacher explained the following to his sixth-grade class:

> The Constitution gives us rights. For example, we have the right to say what we want and to choose our friends. . . .
>
> . . . That our rights are listed on paper means nothing. For our rights to truly matter, we must exercise and protect them.

The three dots at the beginning of the second quoted paragraph indicate the omission of the beginning of that paragraph ("Rights are great, but"). For some types of writing, the convention would require brackets around the capital *T* in the word *That* because *that* was not capitalized in the original sentence. Brackets are discussed in Section XIII.

Note for Lawyers: *The Bluebook* and *The Redbook* recommend slightly different methods for indicating the omission of full paragraphs from multi-paragraph quotes. When writing for courts or publications that do not state a preference, choose the method that you prefer.

5. Spacing Before and After Ellipsis Points

When only three dots are involved, a space typically precedes the first dot and follows the last dot. When four dots are involved, a space typically follows the last dot.

Conventions vary regarding whether to insert a space before the first of four dots.[21] To simplify matters when four dots are involved, we recommend that you insert a space after the last dot but not before the first dot—unless you need to follow a convention that requires otherwise.

EXAMPLES: Spacing of Ellipsis Points

- **Full Quote**
  Glenna said, "The pizza looked divine. It had golden crust and fresh mozzarella. However, the sauce had too much tomato paste, and it gave me heartburn."

- **Four Versus Three Dots**
  Glenna said, "The pizza looked divine. . . . However, the sauce . . . gave me heartburn."

B. Ellipsis Points Signifying a Long Pause or Incompleteness

You can use ellipsis points to signify a long pause or the incompleteness of a thought.

EXAMPLES: **Long Pause and Incompleteness**

- **Long Pause**
  Phoenix stared at the roulette table for what seemed like an hour . . . then placed his chips on a red square.

- **Incompleteness**
  After the argument, the furious wife left the house and went to. . . actually, where she went doesn't matter.

Too many sets of ellipsis points on a page can be distracting or confusing. Thus, we recommend that you sparingly use ellipsis points to signify a pause or incompleteness.

XII. PARENTHESES

A. Nonessential Information

You could use parentheses ( ) to enclose information that furnishes some sort of commentary or detail that is not essential to your main point.

EXAMPLES: **Nonessential Information**

- Tina bought a new car and gave her old one (which is red) to her nephew.
- Paul played Scrabble with Laura (his wife).

Too many parentheses on a page can distract the reader. For that reason, we recommend that you use them judiciously. In some cases, depending on the writer's intended meaning, commas or dashes could substitute for parentheses.

B. Numbered or Lettered List Items in a Sentence

When using numbers or letters to mark list items within a sentence, enclose each number or letter in parentheses.

EXAMPLE: **Numbered List in Sentence**

- Kevin plans to (1) graduate from law school, (2) pass the bar exam, and (3) get a job.

C. Abbreviations and Short Forms

Use parentheses to enclose an abbreviation or short form.

EXAMPLES: **Abbreviation and Short Form**

- Pat worked for the U.S. Securities and Exchange Commission (SEC).
- The Defendant, Adams Construction, Inc. (Corporation), signed a contract with the Plaintiff.

D. Period and Parentheses

If parenthetical material ends a sentence but is not the entire sentence, put the **period outside** the parentheses. If the entire sentence is enclosed in parentheses, put the **period inside** the parentheses.

EXAMPLES: **Periods and Parentheses**

- Stan and Chris went to the theater (they see plays often).
- Marcy ate a salad for lunch. (She is a vegetarian.)

XIII. SQUARE BRACKETS

Square brackets [ ] are commonly used to indicate that material was added to a direct quote, usually as commentary or an explanation.

EXAMPLE: **Inserted Words**

The scientist said, "Most of them [prescription drugs] do have harmful side effects."

The square brackets indicate that the scientist did not actually say *prescription drugs*. The writer inserted those words into the quote to clarify the scientist's use of *them*.

Square brackets also indicate that the first letter of a quote was changed to either uppercase or lowercase.

EXAMPLE: **Capital Letter Changed to Lowercase**

The company insisted that "[r]esearch costs are what cause high drug prices."

The square brackets indicate that the *r* was capitalized in the company's original quote. The writer changed the capital *R* to lowercase to fit better within the writer's sentence.

XIV. PUNCTUATION AND CITATIONS

Conventions vary regarding how to punctuate citations. Consult the guide that is appropriate for you. **Note for Lawyers:** Find out the conventions of the court for which you are writing.

XV. EXCLAMATION POINTS

Exclamation points express emotion or emphasis. We know of no good use for exclamation points in legal, business, or technical writing except possibly for quoting speech or dialogue.

For the following reasons, we recommend that you avoid frequent use of exclamation points in other types of writing:

(1) Frequent use diminishes the emphasis that exclamation points are meant to create.

(2) Exclamation points can be distracting.

(3) They can make a writer seem emotional and thus hard to take seriously.

Endnotes for Chapter 2 (Punctuation)

1   *See, e.g.*, Bishop v. Linkway Stores, Inc., 280 Ark. 106, 123 (1983) (discussing a colon in a contract); Baker v. Nat'l Interstate Ins. Co., 180 Cal. App. 4th 1319, 1330-31 (2009) (discussing a semicolon in an insurance policy); McGrill v. State, 82 So. 3d 130, 132 (Fla. Dist. Ct. App. 2012) (discussing commas in a statute); Maxine Co., Inc. v. Brinks's Global Services USA, Inc., 937 N.Y.S.2d 199, 201-02 (2012) (discussing a comma in a contract).

2   N. Pointe Cas. Ins. Co. v. M & S Tractor Services, Inc., 62 So. 3d 1281, 1283 (Fla. Dist. Ct. App. 2011).

3   Lewis v. Carnaggio, 257 S.C. 54, 56-58 (1971).

4   *See, e.g.*, H. Ramsey Fowler, The Little, Brown Handbook 301 (2d. ed. 1983); Cheryl Glenn and Loretta Gray, The Hodges Harbrace Handbook 157 (18th ed., Wadsworth, 2012); Diana Hacker, The Bedford Handbook: Instructor's Annotated Edition 445 (5th ed. 1998); John C. Hodges, Harbrace Handbook of English 148 (1st ed. 1941); Laura G. Kirszner and Stephen R. Mandell, The Holt Handbook 580 (6th ed. 2002).

5   *E.g.*, Cheryl Glenn & Loretta Gray, The Hodges Harbrace Handbook 200-01 (18th ed., Wadsworth, 2012); William Strunk & E.B. White, The Elements of Style 7 (50th Anniversary ed., Pearson Longman, 2009); diana hacker, The Bedford Handbook: Instructor's Annotated Edition 460-62 (5th ed. 1998).

6   *See, e.g.*, Glenn & Loretta Gray, The Hodges Harbrace Handbook 199-201 (18th ed., Wadsworth, 2012); William Strunk & E.B. White, The Elements of Style 7-8 (50th Anniversary ed. 2009); Diana Hacker, The Bedford Handbook: Instructor's Annotated Edition, 460-62 (5th ed. 1998)

7   University of Chicago Press, The Chicago Manual of Style: The Essential Guide for Writers, Editors, and Publishers 257 (15th ed. 2003).

8   Bryan A. Garner, The Redbook: A Manual on Legal Style 14 (2002); Diana Hacker, The Bedford Handbook: Instructor's Annotated Edition 461 (5th ed. 1998).

9   University of Chicago Press, The Chicago Manual of Style: The Essential Guide for Writers, Editors, and Publishers 61 (15th ed. 2003).

10   William Strunk & E.B. White, The Elements of Style 8 (50th Anniversary ed. 2009).

11   The Bluebook: A Uniform System of Citation 76-77 (Columbia Law Review Ass'n et al. eds., 19th ed. 2010).

12   *E.g.*, Cheryl Glenn & Loretta Gray, The Hodges Harbrace Handbook 140 (18th ed., Wadsworth, 2012) (stating that italics should be used to indicate a word referred to as a word); University of Chicago Press, The Chicago Manual of Style: The Essential Guide for Writers, Editors, and Publishers 294 (15th ed. 2003) (stating that either italics or quotation marks can be used to indicate that a word is being referred to as a word); Bryan A. Garner, The Redbook: A Manual on Legal Style 18 (2002) (stating that either italics or quotation marks can be used to indicate that a word is being referred to as a word).

13   *E.g.*, Cheryl Glenn & Loretta Gray, The Hodges Harbrace Handbook 190 (18th ed., Wadsworth, 2012); University of Chicago Press, The Chicago Manual of Style: The Essential Guide for Writers, Editors, and Publishers 372-75 (15th ed. 2003); Diana Hacker, The Bedford Handbook: Instructor's Annotated Edition 471 (5th ed. 1998).

14   *E.g. Id.*

♦ Endnotes

15 *E.g.*, BRYAN A. GARNER, THE REDBOOK: A MANUAL ON LEGAL STYLE 20 (2002); CHERYL GLENN AND LORETTA GRAY, THE HODGES HARBRACE HANDBOOK 192 (18th ed., Wadsworth, 2012); DIANA HACKER, THE BEDFORD HANDBOOK: INSTRUCTOR'S ANNOTATED EDITION 471 (5th ed. 1998); JOHN C. HODGES, HARBRACE COLLEGE HANDBOOK 154 (4th ed., Harcourt, Brace and Company, 1956); LAURA G. KIRSZNER AND STEPHEN R. MANDELL, THE HOLT HANDBOOK 603 (6th ed. 2002).

16 *E.g.*, BRYAN A. GARNER, THE REDBOOK: A MANUAL ON LEGAL STYLE 20 (2002); CHERYL GLENN AND LORETTA GRAY, THE HODGES HARBRACE HANDBOOK 193 (18th ed., Wadsworth, 2012); DIANA HACKER, THE BEDFORD HANDBOOK: INSTRUCTOR'S ANNOTATED EDITION 472 (5th ed. 1998); JOHN C. HODGES, HARBRACE COLLEGE HANDBOOK 154 (4th ed., Harcourt, Brace and Company, 1956); LAURA G. KIRSZNER AND STEPHEN R. MANDELL, THE HOLT HANDBOOK 603 (6th ed. 2002).

17 *E.g.*, BRYAN A. GARNER, THE REDBOOK: A MANUAL ON LEGAL STYLE 20 (2002); CHERYL GLENN AND LORETTA GRAY, THE HODGES HARBRACE HANDBOOK 193-94 (18th ed., Wadsworth, 2012); DIANA HACKER, THE BEDFORD HANDBOOK: INSTRUC-TOR'S ANNOTATED EDITION 472-73 (5th ed. 1998); JOHN C. HODGES, HARBRACE COLLEGE HANDBOOK 154 (4th ed., Harcourt, Brace and Company, 1956); LAURA G. KIRSZNER AND STEPHEN R. MANDELL, THE HOLT HANDBOOK 604 (6th ed. 2002).

18 UNIVERSITY OF CHICAGO PRESS, THE CHICAGO MANUAL OF STYLE: THE ESSEN-TIAL GUIDE FOR WRITERS, EDITORS, AND PUBLISHERS 458-63 (15th ed. 2003) (the methods are the three-dot method, the three-or-four-dot method, and the rigorous method).

19 *E.g.*, CHERYL GLENN AND LORETTA GRAY, THE HODGES HARBRACE HANDBOOK 207 (18th ed., Wadsworth, 2012); COLUMBIA LAW REVIEW ASSOCIATION, ET AL., THE BLUEBOOK: A UNIFORM SYSTEM OF CITATION 78 (Columbia Law Review Ass'n et al. eds., 19th ed. 2010); UNIVERSITY OF CHICAGO PRESS, THE CHICAGO MANUAL OF STYLE: THE ESSENTIAL GUIDE FOR WRITERS, EDITORS, AND PUBLISHERS 459 (15th ed. 2003); BRYAN A. GARNER, THE REDBOOK: A MANUAL ON LEGAL STYLE 29 (2002); DIANA HACKER, THE BEDFORD HANDBOOK: INSTRUCTOR'S ANNOTATED EDITION 483 (5th ed. 1998); LAURA G. KIRSZNER AND STEPHEN R. MANDELL, THE HOLT HANDBOOK 615 (6th ed. 2002).

20   *E.g.*, University of Chicago Press, The Chicago Manual of Style: The Essential Guide for Writers, Editors, and Publishers 459-61 (15th ed. 2003) (this manual sets out both a method involving three dots and a method involving four dots); Bryan A. Garner, The Redbook: A Manual on Legal Style 28-29 (2002) (this manual recommends using a set of three centered dots on its own line to indicate omission of a paragraph and states that *The Bluebook* recommends a different convention).

21   *E.g.*, University of Chicago Press, The Chicago Manual of Style: The Essential Guide for Writers, Editors, and Publishers 460, 463 (15th ed. 2003) (this manual's "three-or-four-dot method" requires no space before the first of four dots because the first dot is a period; conversely, this manual's "rigorous method" requires a space before the first of the four dots because the fourth dot is the period).

CHAPTER 3.
Style

I. STYLE GENERALLY

STYLE IS SUBJECTIVE. Different people have different ideas of what qualifies as good or bad style. While editing this book, the authors vigorously debated some stylistic points.

Different contexts call for different writing styles. For example, literary writing is expected to be brimming with verbal panache. On the other hand, the focus in technical writing is on accuracy, clarity, and brevity.

In this chapter, we provide basic style tips that promote accurate and clear communication—a good foundation for non-fiction writing in most professional settings. If you are interested in the appropriate style for a different type of writing (e.g., mystery or romance novels), you might consult a book on that subject.

II. AVOID UNINTENDED AMBIGUITY

In the grammatical context, language is ambiguous if it conveys more than one possible meaning. In the legal context, language is ambiguous if it conveys more than one *reasonable* meaning.[1] Ambiguity undermines accurate and clear communication.

♦ Ambiguity

In some contexts, a writer might intend to create ambiguity—for example, relying on double meaning for comic purposes. Unless you have a good reason to create ambiguity, we recommend that you avoid it.

Two common causes of ambiguity are (1) word choice and (2) word placement. The following sets of examples are based on bungled, real-world newspaper headlines.

EXAMPLES: Ambiguity Caused by Word Choice

1. Prostitute <u>Appeals</u> to Governor
2. Children <u>Make</u> Tasty Snacks

<u>Headline 1</u>: One possible meaning is that the prostitute lobbied the governor; the other meaning is that the governor finds the prostitute appealing.

<u>Headline 2</u>: One possible meaning is that the children prepared tasty snacks; the other meaning is that children are good to eat.

EXAMPLES: Ambiguity Caused by Word Placement

1. Criticism about Models <u>Growing Ugly</u>
2. Woman Punches Man <u>in her Nightgown</u>

<u>Headline 1</u>: One possible meaning is that the criticism is growing ugly; the other meaning is that the models are.

Headline 2: One possible meaning is that the woman was wearing her nightgown; the other meaning is that the man was.

Recognizing and resolving ambiguity is further discussed in Chapter 1, Sections IV.D and VII.

III. STRIVE FOR SIMPLICITY

A. Simplicity and Clarity

Simplicity tends to promote clarity. A sentence is clear if it is easy to understand. The indiscriminate use of convoluted sentences or grandiose words makes text hard to follow.

When possible, a writer intending to clearly convey information should use common words and simple sentence structure. The adequate expression of some concepts might require technical or esoteric terms. The accurate handling of some concepts might require more complex sentences than the handling of other concepts. The key is to choose simplicity over *needless* complexity.

Tips for Achieving Simplicity

- Choose common terms over needlessly technical or esoteric terms (Section III.B).

- Choose a simpler sentence structure over a needlessly complex structure (Section III.C).

- Break a needlessly lengthy sentence into multiple shorter ones (Section III.D).

♦ Simplicity

Note for Lawyers: Courts have criticized needlessly complex language in legal documents,[2] and states' legislative drafting manuals generally recommend simplicity.[3]

B. Choose Common Terms When Possible

When possible, choose a common word over a grandiose one. If Michael *chewed* food, why write that he *masticated*? If you mean *house*, why write *habitation* or *residence*? If the word *use* conveys your meaning, why write *utilize*—which means the same thing except in limited contexts?[4]

That is not to say that you should always choose the common word. In some cases, the grander-sounding word is more accurate. For example, *homestead* is a better choice than *home* for a writer describing farmland containing a house and all of the outbuildings on the land.[5] The key is to choose the common word over a grandiose word that does not better reflect your intended meaning.

C. Use Simple Sentence Structure

Simple sentence structure makes the reader's task easy. Needlessly complex phrasing or sentence structure (1) increases the reader's burden and (2) can create confusion and ambiguity.

A very simple sentence structure looks like this:

Subject ⇨ verb ⇨ completion of thought.

By "completion of thought," we mean an element (e.g., a prepositional phrase or a direct object) without which the sentence would lack
information.

EXAMPLES: **Simple Sentences**
(completion of thought underlined)

- Gabriella bought <u>new tires</u>.
  subj.   *verb*
- Kirsten worked <u>at the courthouse</u>.
  subj.   *verb*

As illustrated in the next subsection, some details could be added to a
simple sentence without making the sentence hard for the reader to grasp
in one reading. The key is to refrain from adding so many details that the
sentence structure becomes needlessly complex and forces the reader to
reread the sentence to figure out what it means.

D. Avoid Overloading Your Sentences

An overloaded sentence is needlessly packed with information, some
of which could easily go into a different sentence. Forcing an overloaded
sentence on a reader is like cramming a whole pizza into someone's mouth:
it's overwhelming and hard to digest. Thus, we recommend that you avoid
inflicting overloaded sentences on your readers.

Note for Lawyers: Courts have criticized overloaded sentences in legal documents.[6]

A sentence should be digestible in a single reading. Generally, a sentence expressing one thought is easier to digest than a sentence expressing many thoughts. One guideline (not a firm rule) for preventing sentence-overload is to limit sentences to the following if possible:

- Only one major actor.

- Only one major verb.

- Only a manageable number of details.

How many details qualify as a "manageable number"? The number depends on the complexity of the details and where you place them in the sentence. Even one detail could be unmanageable if it is lengthy and puts too much distance between the core sentence's key elements (e.g., the subject and its verb). Placing 20 words between a subject and its verb would probably prompt readers to either reread the sentence or skip past it. Placing two words between a subject and its verb would probably not confuse readers.

Consider the three sentences below, all of which contain the same core sentence (Sentence 1). Sentences 2 and 3 contain the core sentence's elements (bold) plus additional details.

1. **The city attorney moved into the house next door.**

2. On June 10, 2013, following her resignation, **the city attorney moved into the house next door** to my grandmother's house.

3. On June 10, 2013, following her resignation due to widespread public criticism of her handling of the Frazier case, **the city attorney**, a former family friend who had fallen out with my grandmother over the city's enforcement of a previously never-enforced zoning regulation, **moved**, presumably enticed by its extremely low price, **into the house**, which everyone in town believed to be haunted and which had been standing empty for 20 years, **next door** to my grandmother's house.

Sentence 2 is easy to follow, though it is longer than Sentence 1. Sentence 2 contains the core sentence plus three details (date, resignation, and grandmother's house). Sentence 2 is digestible because it contains only one major actor; one major verb; and a manageable number of details, which are placed so that the core sentence's elements are together.

Sentence 3 is a "whole pizza." To form Sentence 3, we added more than ten details to the core sentence. We used six modifying phrases or clauses and threw in a confusing number of commas. We also placed those details in a way that separates the core sentence's elements from each other, making it hard to keep track of the sentence's point.

To make the story easier to follow, we could easily use four sentences to express the content of Sentence 3:

- Due to widespread public criticism of her handling of the Frazier case, the city attorney resigned.

- On June 10, 2013, the city attorney moved into the house next door to my grandmother's house.

- A former family friend, the city attorney had fallen out with my grandmother over the city's enforcement of a previously never-enforced zoning regulation.

- Presumably the city attorney was enticed by the house's extremely low price; the house, which everyone in town believed to be haunted, had been standing empty for 20 years.

How to break up an overloaded sentence is a judgment call. For example, different writers might use five or six sentences to cover Sentence 3's content and might order the sentences differently. Similarly, one writer might organize the sentences into two paragraphs, and another might use three. The point is that the original Sentence 3 is severely overloaded, and solving the problem requires using multiple sentences.

As discussed in Section III, some sentences must be long because they convey complex or necessarily detailed information. Other sentences are long and burdensome for no reason other than that the writer did not break them up.

IV. WRITE CONCISELY

Every minute that a reader spends laboring to read unnecessary words is a minute of life that the reader loses forever. In short, wordiness wastes time, which can irritate readers and even cause them to stop reading. Thus, we recommend that you write concisely.

A concise sentence contains no *unnecessary* words. Conciseness is not about deleting words to merely save space: it is about deleting words that do not serve the writer's purpose. (If the split infinitive in the prior sentence troubles you, see Chapter 1, Section VIII.)

EXAMPLES: **Deletion of Unnecessary Words**
(unnecessary words underlined)

1(a)   The trip was a long one.   (6 words)

1(b)   The trip was long.   (4 words)

2(a)   The fact is that the car was   (16 words)
       bought by Brett on the 5th
       day of July.

2(b)   Brett bought the car on July 5.   (7 words)

Because words and phrases are the building blocks of a sentence, one way to achieve conciseness is to choose shorter words or phrases that say the same thing as their longer counterparts. Consider the following examples:

♦ Conciseness

Less Concise	More concise
subsequent to	after
prior to	before
at the present time	now (or presently)
due to the fact that	because
in spite of the fact that	though (or although)
the State of Vermont	Vermont
in the month of June	in June
on the fifth day of May	on May 5
yellow in color	yellow
six in number	six
a distance of ten miles	ten miles

A **noun's possessive form** is usually more concise than phrasing that relies on *of* to show possession.

EXAMPLES: **Possessive Form vs. *Of*-Phrasing**

1(a) The tenth birthday of Catherine...   (5 words)

1(b) Catherine's tenth birthday...   (3 words)

2(a) Judge Jones read the notes of the Appropriations Committee of the Senate of the United States.   (16 words)

2(b) Judge Jones read the United States Senate's Appropriations Committee's notes.   (10 words)

In some cases, an **adjective** is a concise substitute for a prepositional phrase.

EXAMPLE: **Adjective versus Prepositional Phrase**

A document of a legislative nature.   (6 words)

A legislative document.   (3 words)

An **active-voice sentence** is more concise than a passive-voice sentence that names the agent.

EXAMPLES: **Relative Wordiness of Passive Voice**
(extra words underlined)

1(a) **Passive:** A book <u>was</u> read <u>by</u> Sookie.   (6 words)

1(b) **Active:** Sookie read a book.   (4 words)

2(a) **Passive:** A gift <u>was</u> received <u>by</u> Tara.   (6 words)

2(b) **Active:** Tara received a gift.   (4 words)

Unnecessary details undermine conciseness. Whether a detail is unnecessary depends on the context. We recommend that you carefully consider which details in a sentence serve a purpose and which details you could omit while still conveying the relevant information.

Redundancy, the needless repetition of information or use of words, also undermines conciseness. Unless you have a good reason to remind the reader of a point, we recommend that you avoid repeating information. Instead of writing a string of synonyms, choose the word that accurately conveys your intended meaning.

EXAMPLE: **String of Synonyms**

The victim expected to be <u>paid</u>, <u>compensated</u>, and <u>recompensed</u> for his injuries.

In the example, any one of the three underlined verbs would suffice. Given the resources available (e.g., online dictionaries and thesauruses), it is easy to avoid redundancy.

Note for Lawyers: in the spirit of covering all bases, lawyers sometimes string together synonyms. If the synonyms have overlapping—but not exactly the same—meanings, doing so can be sensible and would not necessarily create redundancy. We recommend that you avoid stringing together synonyms unless a synonym string has a special meaning in the law or serves a worthwhile purpose.

V. AVOID PASSIVE VOICE UNLESS YOU NEED IT

Passive voice can be useful, as discussed in Chapter 1. Two good reasons for using passive voice are (1) to emphasize the verb or its object and (2) to de-emphasize (or omit) the actor.

We recommend that you avoid using passive voice unless you have a good reason for using it. Passive-voice sentences that do not name the actor tend to be unclear. Passive-voice sentences that name the actor are less concise than active-voice sentences.

Note for Lawyers: In legal documents, an actor's responsibility is usually a central concern. Thus, we recommend that legal writers avoid using passive voice unless the actor's identity is unknown, irrelevant, or better left unexpressed. Many states' legislative-drafting manuals similarly advise against the needless use of passive voice.[7]

VI. CHOOSE WORDS THAT BEST REFLECT YOUR MEANING

To express yourself clearly and accurately, choose words that reflect your exact meaning. As Mark Twain advised, "Use the right word, not its second cousin."

Some English words have related meanings, yet their definitions differ somewhat. Instead of choosing a word that seems to be "in the ballpark" of your intended meaning, consult a thesaurus. After you know your options, look up those words in a dictionary, then choose the one that best reflects your intended meaning. Consider the following examples:

- *Pay*: to give money to someone for a service, a good, or a debt.

- *Reimburse*: to pay someone in order to make up for a loss or expense.

- *Remunerate*: to pay someone for services rendered.

Be aware of a word's connotations (i.e., the ideas or feelings associated with it), as well as the dictionary meaning. For example, consider the different connotations of the following pairs of words:

- *Statesman* and *politician.*

- *Challenged* and *handicapped.*

- *Teach* and *indoctrinate.*

The first word of each pair has a more positive connotation than the second. For example, *statesman* suggests an honorable and respect-worthy person. *Politician* suggests a person who is not so honorable or deserving of respect.

Dictionaries and thesauruses are available on the Internet and come pre-installed in many computers. Those electronic resources are quick, making it easy for you to choose the words that best reflect your intended meaning.

VII. AVOID NEEDLESS JARGON

A. About Jargon Generally

Jargon is the specialized language of a profession or group. Jargon can be useful because it can clearly and concisely convey complex concepts to readers who understand the jargon. For example, it would be more concise for an economist writing an article for other economists to use the word *oligopoly* than to continually repeat a phrase such as "a state in which a few sellers control the market for a product."

Jargon does not always make a writer seem sophisticated. Sometimes needless jargon makes a writer seem pretentious or lazy about editing. We recommend that you avoid using jargon unless it makes your meaning easier for your intended audience to grasp.

B. About Legal Jargon

Some legal terms are necessary in some legal documents.[8] For example, some types of contracts necessarily include terms such as *liquidated damages* or *warranty of merchantability.*

However, many esoteric modifiers and prepositions—to which some lawyers seem addicted—are usually not necessary. Even worse, such words and phrases can overburden readers and reduce clarity.

EXAMPLES: **(Usually) Needless Terms in Legal Writing**

Aforementioned	Hereinafter
And/or	Hereinbefore
Any and all	Monies (it's all *money*)
By and through	Notwithstanding
Foregoing	Said (meaning *the*)
Forthwith	Such (meaning *the*)
Herein	Subsequent to

We recommend that you omit needless legal jargon from your writing. We are in good company: many states' legislative-drafting manuals advise drafters to avoid needless legal jargon,[9] and a recent study suggests that many judges prefer documents written in plain English over those written in "legalese."[10]

Some busy lawyers blindly copy language from sample documents without fully considering the meaning of that language. If you see legal jargon in a sample document, don't assume that the language was included for good reasons—and don't assume that the language can be edited without changing the meaning.

Instead, do some research regarding any terms of questionable meaning. If the jargon is necessary and reflects your intended meaning, then use it. If not, try to phrase your provisions without the jargon.

VIII. USE GENDER-NEUTRAL NOUNS AND PRONOUNS

Accuracy is one reason for writing gender-neutrally any statements intended to apply equally to males and females. Another reason is that some readers, including business associates, might take exception to gender-specific language. Why risk offending anyone when it is so easy to eliminate the potential problem?

One way to achieve gender-neutrality is to choose gender-neutral nouns and pronouns. Below are examples of gender-specific nouns and their gender-neutral substitutes:

Gender-Specific	**Gender-Neutral**
Businessman	Businessperson
Chairman	Chairperson, Chair
Fireman	Firefighter
Foreman	Supervisor
Mailman	Mail carrier
Policeman, policewoman	Police officer
Salesman, saleswoman	Salesperson
Waiter, Waitress	Server
Workman	Worker

One way to achieve gender-neutrality with respect to pronouns is to omit pronouns altogether and to repeat the antecedent instead. The omission of pronouns also eliminates the potential for two types of errors: (1) pronoun-related ambiguity and (2) pronoun-case errors.

On the other hand, repetition of the antecedent can make a sentence sound awkward, which would not work well for writers whose goals include a smooth or elegant style (e.g. fiction writers). Repetition of the antecedent is more useful to writers who prioritize precision over style (e.g. legal or technical writers).

Note for Lawyers: It is widely agreed[11] that legal documents should be drafted gender-neutrally (1) when gender is not relevant or (2) when the drafter does not know the subject's gender. If you insist on using pronouns in legal documents, you can achieve gender-neutrality by using phrases such as "he, she, or it"; "him, her, or it"; and "his, hers, or its." Many readers would find such phrasing cumbersome, but the choice is yours.

If you use pronouns, use them correctly. As discussed in Chapter 1, pronouns must agree in number (singular vs. plural) with their antecedents. *They*, *them*, and *their* are gender-neutral, but it is incorrect and potentially confusing to use a plural pronoun to refer to a singular antecedent.

IX. TRANSITIONAL LANGUAGE

Creating transitions between sentences can enhance clarity. One way to create a transition is through transitional language: i.e., a word or phrase that signifies how one sentence relates to another.

EXAMPLES: **Transitional Words and Phrases**

However	For example
Therefore (or thus)	In addition
Consequently	In contrast
Nevertheless	As a result
Furthermore	For the most part
Conversely	On the other hand

We have two recommendations regarding transitional language:

(1) Use it correctly.

(2) Do not overuse it.

The incorrect use of transitional language undermines the writer's intended meaning. The overuse of transitional language can make writing sound repetitive or stilted, as though generated by a robot that is programmed to strictly follow a template.

How much transitional language is too much? That is a judgment call. One factor is the type of writing involved. For example, transitional language probably should have a stronger presence in argumentative writing than in some forms of technical writing. The key to effectively using transitional language is to use it for a good reason, not gratuitously.

X. STRIVE FOR CONNECTEDNESS

When sentences in a paragraph are connected, readers have an easier time following the writer's message. When editing, check your sentences for connectedness. Does each sentence follow logically from the preceding sentence? For example, does the second sentence in your paragraph continue the same topic as the first or introduce a new topic? If the latter, does the new topic relate to information introduced in the previous sentence?

To build connectedness, link your sentences through consistent terminology. If you intend the same meaning, use the same word. For example, if a paragraph's first sentence refers to a residence as a *house*, then continue using *house* in later sentences in that paragraph. If a paragraph refers to a specific person as a *scientist*, continue in later paragraphs to use *scientist* when referring to that person.

XI. INDENTED LISTS

A. When to Indent Lists

Some sentences address a list of choices or requirements. Indented lists allow a writer to deal with details that would otherwise create an overloaded sentence. Overloaded sentences are discussed in Section III.D.

An indented list visually sets off the list items so that the reader can easily see the items and grasp how they all relate to the list's introductory clause. As long as you do not overuse indented lists, they can make the reader's task easier by highlighting a sentence's components.

What qualifies as overuse of indented lists? That is a judgment call. We recommend that you avoid putting one indented list directly after another if only a few lines of text are between the two lists. Too many indented lists on a page can distract readers.

Indented formatting is **not necessary for small lists** and takes up more room on the page than non-indented formatting.

EXAMPLES: **Small Lists**

1. Mike liked the following sports: football, soccer, and basketball.

2. Mike liked the following sports:
   • football,
   • soccer, and
   • basketball.

It would *not* be incorrect to indent the small list in the examples above, but indenting is not necessary given how easy it is to read that simple list in a non-indented format.

B. Characteristics of Indented Lists

Generally, a list should be introduced by an independent clause. Each list item should directly relate to the introductory clause. A well-written indented list, such as the one below, has the following characteristics:

(1) All list items are equally indented.

(2) All list items are grammatically parallel (see Chapter 1, Section VI).

(3) Each list item works grammatically if read together with the introductory clause.

(4) Each list item is lettered, numbered, or bulleted (in legal documents, each item should be lettered or numbered for easy referencing).

(5) All list items are properly punctuated.

Some writers do not use an independent clause or a colon to introduce a list if each list item completes the introductory phrase. The following is an example:

A user of the campground shall not

(a) build a fire anywhere except in the designated area,

(b) park a vehicle anywhere except in the designated area, or

(c) leave behind litter in any area.

One author of this book is comfortable using the type of list illustrated directly above. The other author prefers to use an independent clause, followed by a colon, to introduce a list. Both ways are acceptable.

C. Punctuating Indented Lists

Conventions for punctuating indented lists vary, and different types of writers (e.g., technical or legal) may follow different conventions. If you are not following a specific convention for punctuating indented lists, you could choose one of the following options:

(1) begin each list item with a capital letter, and end it with a period; **or**

(2) begin each item with a lower-case letter, end it with a comma or semicolon (whichever is appropriate), and place an *and* or an *or* after the next-to-last list item.

ENDNOTES FOR CHAPTER 3 (STYLE)

1   *E.g.*, Bourke v. Dun & Bradstreet Corp., 159 F.3d 1032, 1036 (7th Cir. 1998) (apply-ing Illinois law, the court states that an instrument is ambiguous if the language is "rea-sonably or fairly susceptible to having more than one meaning"); Burger King Corp. v. Horn & Hardart Co., 893 F.2d 525, 527 (2d Cir. 1990) (the court states, "Contract language is ambiguous if it is reasonably susceptible of more than one interpretation, and a court makes this determination by reference to the contract alone"); Watkins v. Petro-Search, Inc., 689 F.2d 537, 538 (5th Cir. 1982) (applying Texas law, the court states, "A contract is ambiguous when it is reasonably susceptible to more than one meaning, in the light of the surrounding circumstances and after applying established rules of construction").

2   *E.g.*, N. Pointe Cas. Ins. Co. v. M & S Tractor Services, Inc., 62 So. 3d 1281, 1283-85 (Fla. Dist. Ct. App. 2011) (finding ambiguity due to, among other things, convoluted sentence structure); Midland Funding, LLC v. Layton, No. 09-464-CC, 2009 WL 6813116 (Fla. Cir. Ct. Mar. 20, 2009) (criticizing plaintiff's use of "hundred-dollar words" in a pleading); Ramos-Barrientos v. Bland, No. 606CV089, 2008 WL 474426, at *1-2 (S.D. Ga. Feb. 19, 2008) (criticizing convoluted and lengthy sentences in a plead-ing).

3   *E.g.*, DELAWARE LEGISLATIVE COUNCIL DIVISION OF RESEARCH, DRAFTING DEL-AWARE LEGISLATION 1 (2009) (advising drafters (1) to use short, simple sentences be-cause complex sentence structures can cause ambiguity; and (2) to try to keep sentence length at or below 21 words); KENTUCKY LEGISLATIVE RESEARCH COMMISSION, BILL DRAFTING MANUAL 23-24 (2011) (stating that simplicity is "highly desirable" if it does not cause loss of meaning and advising selection of short, familiar words if possible); MARYLAND DEPARTMENT OF LEGISLATIVE SERVICES, LEGISLATIVE DRAFTING MAN-UAL 26 (2012) (advising drafters (1) to avoid long sentences; (2) to use short, familiar words and phrases; and (3) to not use multiple words if one word suffices).

4   *E.g.*, H. W. FOWLER, A DICTIONARY OF MODERN ENGLISH USAGE 473-75 (edited by Sir Ernest Gowers, 2d ed., 1965) (stating that *utilize* was distinct from *use* but that the distinction has been lost and that *utilize* became merely a longer version of *use*); WIL-LIAM STRUNK, JR. AND E.B. WHITE, THE ELEMENTS OF STYLE 77-78 (50th Anniversary ed., Pearson Longman, 2009) (stating a preference for *use* over *utilize*).

5   NEW OXFORD AMERICAN DICTIONARY 809 (2nd ed., 2005).

6   *See, e.g.*, Stanard v. Nygren, 658 F.3d 792, 798 (7th Cir. 2011) ("At least 23 sentences contained 100 or more words. This includes sentences of 385, 345, and 291 words"); Midland Funding, LLC v. Layton, No. 09-464-CC, 2009 WL 6813116 (Fla. Cir. Ct. Mar. 20, 2009) ("[C]onsider this 68-word, no-comma sentence from paragraph 19 of the complaint...").

7   *E.g.*, ARIZONA LEGISLATIVE COUNCIL, THE ARIZONA LEGISLATION BILL DRAFT-ING MANUAL 87 (2009); FLORIDA SENATE, MANUAL FOR DRAFTING LEGISLATION 12 (6ᵗʰ ed. 2009); INDIANA GENERAL ASSEMBLY, BILL DRAFTING MANUAL, *available at* http://www.in.gov/legislative/2367.htm; LEGISLATIVE COUNCIL OF THE MAINE STATE LEGISLATURE, MAINE LEGISLATIVE DRAFTING MANUAL 77 (2009); TEXAS LEGISLA-TIVE COUNCIL, DRAFTING MANUAL 102 (2011).

8   *E.g.*, Patton v. State, 34 So. 3d 563, 574-75 (Miss. 2010) (stating that "a properly drafted false pretense indictment is replete with essential legalese, long required by this Court, that would be unfamiliar to most attorneys, even law professors, other than those with significant experience as prosecutors, criminal defense attorneys or judges in Mississippi's criminal courts").

9   *See, e.g.*, FLORIDA HOUSE OF REPRESENTATIVES, GUIDELINES FOR BILL DRAFTING 95 (2011); LEGISLATIVE COUNCIL OF THE MAINE STATE LEGISLATURE, MAINE LEG-ISLATIVE DRAFTING MANUAL 104 (2009); TEXAS LEGISLATIVE COUNCIL, DRAFTING MANUAL 106 (2011).

10   Sean Flammer, *A New Comprehensive Study Confirms that Judges Find Plain English More Persuasive than Legalese*, 90 Mich. B.J. 50, 50-51 (2011).

11   *E.g.*, N.H. REV. STAT. ANN. § 17-A:6 (2012) (encouraging the use of gender-neutral terms in drafting legislation); OHIO ADMIN. CODE 103-3-02 (2012) (encouraging agen-cies to draft rules using gender-neutral language); STATE OF CONNECTICUT, MANUAL FOR DRAFTING REGULATIONS 46 (2009) (advising drafters to draft gender-neutrally); FLORIDA SENATE, MANUAL FOR DRAFTING LEGISLATION 13 (6th ed. 2009) (advising drafters to avoid gender-specific pronouns); TEXAS LEGISLATIVE COUNCIL, TEXAS LEGISLATIVE COUNCIL DRAFTING MANUAL 103 (2011) (stating that drafters should express ideas in gender-neutral terms if possible); Gerald Lebovits, *Ethical Judicial Writing—Part III*, 79 N.Y. St. B.J. 64, 64 (2007) (stating that New York requires that court opinions be gender-neutral).

APPENDIX 1
Exercises for Self-Testing

I. KEY GRAMMATICAL TERMS

Answer the questions about each of the following sentences.

Sentence 1: Three tall men walked into a bar.

1. What is the main verb?
2. What is the main verb's subject?
3. What is the sentence's subject?
4. What type of phrase is "three tall men"?
5. What type of phrase is "into a bar"?

Sentence 2: Will threw the ball to the wide receiver.

1. What is the main verb?
2. What is the main verb's subject?
3. What is the sentence's subject?
4. What is the sentence's predicate?

5. Which part of speech is the word "to"?

6. Which type of phrase is "to the wide receiver"?

7. What is the direct object of the verb "threw"?

Sentence 3: After Stacey wrote the brief, she ate lunch.

1. What is the sentence's subject?

2. Which type of clause is "after Stacey wrote the brief"?

3. Which type of clause is "she ate lunch"?

4. What is the direct object of the verb "wrote"?

5. What is the direct object of the verb "ate"?

Sentence 4: Diane prepared a meal, ate the meal, and washed the dishes.

1. What are the three verbs?

2. What is the direct object of "prepared"?

3. What is the direct object of "ate"?

4. What is the direct object of "washed"?

5. The word "the" is an article: what part of speech is it?

6. What part of speech is the word "and"?

Sentence 5: Finishing the project will be difficult.

1. What is the verb?

2. What is the verb's subject? *(Gerunds function as nouns)*

3. Which part of speech is "difficult"?

II. VOICE OF VERBS

Answer the following questions about the underlined verb or verb phrase in each of the following sentences:

A. Is it transitive or intransitive?

B. Is it in active voice, passive voice, or no voice?

1.   The dog <u>was</u> tired.
2.   The dog <u>was walked</u>.
3.   The man <u>had eaten</u> the whole pizza.
4.   The whole pizza <u>had been eaten</u> by the man.
5.   Pat <u>bought</u> the business.
6.   The business <u>was bought</u> by Pat.
7.   The business <u>was bought</u>.
8.   Greg <u>was swimming</u>.
9.   Greg <u>will swim</u> tomorrow.
10.   Greg <u>will be swimming</u> tomorrow.
11.   The CEO's assistant <u>is shredding</u> the files.
12.   The files <u>are being shredded</u>.
13.   The decision <u>was made</u>.
14.   Bert <u>jogged</u> for an hour.
15.   Tanya <u>will be</u> late.

III. PRONOUNS

A. Number

If an underlined pronoun is incorrect, replace it with the correct one.

1. An intoxicated person should not drive <u>their</u> car.
2. If a customer returns merchandise, the store will give <u>them</u> a refund.
3. Pregnant women need <u>their</u> rest.
4. The company revised <u>their</u> financial statements.
5. The court published <u>their</u> opinion in the Tomlinson case.

B. Ambiguous Usage

Choose one party as the ambiguously used pronoun's antecedent and rewrite each sentence so that the meaning is clear. Assume that gender is correct.

1. The bottle hit the window, and <u>it</u> broke.
2. Hayden checked the numbers and told John that <u>he</u> had won the state lottery.
3. The dog chased the cat until <u>he</u> stopped.
4. The department heads told the managers that <u>they</u> needed to give budgetary information to the CEO.
5. If a corporation disputes the Agency's decision, <u>it</u> must disclose all relevant information.

C. Case

If an underlined pronoun is incorrect, replace it with the correct one. Assume that gender is correct.

1. Betsy went to lunch with Diane and <u>I</u>.

2. For <u>who</u> did the bell toll?

3. Did the bell toll for <u>she</u> or <u>he</u>?

4. We sent the notice to <u>yours</u> and <u>their</u> attorneys.

5. The letter was sent to Andy and <u>me</u> concerning the person <u>who</u> the Board is considering for the position.

6. Mary felt sorry for the lawyer <u>who</u> the judge had held in contempt.

7. <u>Who</u> besides <u>he</u> did the seller notify?

8. If <u>they</u> do not get involved, what will happen to <u>he</u> and <u>I</u>?

9. <u>Whom</u> was the person <u>who</u> had custody of the dog when it chased my brother and <u>me</u>?

10. The judge greeted my partner and <u>I</u>.

IV. PUNCTUATION

A. Spotting Punctuation Errors

Circle any comma, semi-colon, colon, or apostrophe that is <u>incorrectly used</u> in the following sentences.

1. Nancy bought an emerald ring; but she was dissatisfied with it's setting, and returned it.

2. "I am dissatisfied", Nancy said to the store manager.

3. Ted bought a novel, and read it in a day.

4. Lindsay drove to the campus, but she could not find a parking spot.

5. Three people spoke at the meeting: Emily, an attorney, Katie, a writer, and Sara, a film director.

B. Adding Punctuation

Where appropriate, add a comma, semicolon, apostrophe or period. If a sentence requires no additional punctuation, write NPR.

1. During his teenage years Rod saw only three bands perform on stage Pink Floyd The Who and Led Zeppelin his favorite band

2. You have to go to the dentist Twyla said to her son I don't want to go the boy replied

3. After putting away the childrens toys the babysitter fed the dog made lunch and settled in front of the TV

4. Its a wonderful world Sandra thought as she watched her puppy chase its toy

5. After spending a week in Miami Victorina went to Madrid Barcelona and Paris she enjoyed her vacation

V. SIMPLICITY AND CONCISENESS

A. Words and Phrases

Write a simpler or more concise substitute for each of the underlined words and phrases.

1. Kathleen spoke <u>in a pleasant manner</u>.

2. <u>In the event that</u> Cal is sick, he will not go to work.

3. Ron wrote the book <u>in conjunction with</u> Harriet.

4. Caroline <u>made an inquiry about</u> the school's rules.

5. Josh <u>ameliorated</u> his grade by doing extra-credit work.

6. Jennifer <u>utilized</u> a computer to write her novel.

7. Henry proposed to Rebecca <u>in the month of February</u>.

8. Maggie made her car payments <u>on a monthly basis</u>.

9. Joy is driving to the store <u>at the present time</u>.

10. Scott left his job <u>due to the fact that</u> he hated it.

11. The murder trial <u>commenced</u> on Monday.

12. The City will accept bids <u>subsequent to</u> July 10.

13. Cassie went shopping <u>prior to</u> Christmas.

14. The lion hunted <u>in order to</u> survive.

15. Mick <u>endeavored</u> to write a song.

B. Sentences

Make the following sentences as simple and concise as you can without changing the essence.

1. Gifts were received by Jennifer, on the fifth anniversary of her birth, from her mother and father.

2. Tracy planned to make a donation, in the form of a monetary contribution, to an organization that was engaged in charitable activities.

3. Albert is a man who enjoys reading and has a preference for authors who write concisely by using no more words than are absolutely necessary to convey the intended message.

4. Bart served, throughout all of the year 2012, as the chairman of the budget committee of the club, which committee (as suggested by its name) was responsible for dealing with issues relating to the club's budget.

5. Huge bonuses were paid by the company, despite the fact that substantial losses were reported by the company and despite the fact that the company had decided that it was necessary to lay off a significant number of individuals who were employed by the company, to executive-level employees.

APPENDIX 2

Answers to Exercises

I. KEY GRAMMATICAL TERMS

Answer the questions about each of the following sentences.

Sentence 1: Three tall men walked into a bar.

1. What is the main verb?
   Walked.

2. What is the main verb's subject?
   Three tall men.

3. What is the sentence's subject?
   Three tall men.

4. What type of phrase is "three tall men"?
   Noun phrase.

5. What type of phrase is "into a bar"?
   Prepositional phrase.

Sentence 2: Will threw the ball to the wide receiver.

1. What is the main verb?
   Threw.

2. What is the main verb's subject?
   Will.

3. What is the sentence's subject?
   Will.

4. What is the sentence's predicate?
   Threw the ball to the wide receiver.

5.   Which part of speech is the word "to"?
     Preposition.

6.   Which type of phrase is "to the wide receiver"?
     Prepositional phrase.

7.   What is the direct object of the verb "threw"?
     Ball.

Sentence 3: After Stacey wrote the brief, she ate lunch.

1.   What is the sentence's subject?
     She.

2.   Which type of clause is "after Stacey wrote the brief"?
     Dependent clause.

3.   Which type of clause is "she ate lunch"?
     Independent clause.

4.   What is the direct object of the verb "wrote"?
     Brief.

5.   What is the direct object of the verb "ate"?
     Lunch.

Sentence 4: Diane prepared a meal, ate the meal, and washed the dishes.

1.   What are the three verbs?
     Prepared, ate, and washed.

2.   What is the direct object of "prepared"?
     Meal.

3.   What is the direct object of "ate"?
     Meal.

4.   What is the direct object of "washed"?
     Dishes.

5. The word "the" is an article: what part of speech is it?
   Adjective.

6. What part of speech is the word "and"?
   Conjunction.

Sentence 5: Finishing the project will be difficult.

1. What is the verb?
   Will be.

2. What is the verb's subject? (*Gerunds function as nouns*)
   Finishing.

3. Which part of speech is "difficult"?
   Adjective.

II. VOICE OF VERBS

Answer the following questions about the underlined verb or verb phrase in each of the following sentences:

A. Is it transitive or intransitive?

B. Is it in active voice, passive voice, or no voice?

1. The dog <u>was</u> tired.
   Intransitive, no voice.

2. The dog <u>was walked</u>.
   Transitive, passive voice.

3. The man <u>had eaten</u> the whole pizza.
   Transitive, active voice.

4. The whole pizza <u>had been eaten</u> by the man.
    Transitive, passive voice.

5. Pat <u>bought</u> the business.
    Transitive, active voice.

6. The business <u>was bought</u> by Pat.
    Transitive, passive voice.

7. The business <u>was bought</u>.
    Transitive, passive voice.

8. Greg <u>was swimming</u>.
    Intransitive, no voice.

9. Greg <u>will swim</u> tomorrow.
    Intransitive, no voice.

10. Greg <u>will be swimming</u> tomorrow.
    Intransitive, no voice.

11. The CEO's assistant <u>is shredding</u> the files.
    Transitive, active voice.

12. The files <u>are being shredded</u>.
    Transitive, passive voice.

13. The decision <u>was made</u>.
    Transitive, passive voice.

14. Bert <u>jogged</u> for an hour.
    Intransitive, no voice.

15. Tanya <u>will be</u> late.
    Intransitive, no voice.

III. Pronouns

A. Number

If an underlined pronoun is incorrect, replace it with the correct one.

1. An intoxicated person should not drive their car.
   ***His* or *her*.**

2. If a customer returns merchandise, the store will give them a refund.
   ***Him* or *her* (or *the customer*).**

3. Pregnant women need their rest.
   Correct.

4. The company revised their financial statements.
   ***Its* (or *the company's*).**

5. The court published their opinion in the Tomlinson case.
   ***Its* (or *the court's*).**

B. Ambiguous Usage

Choose one party as the ambiguously used pronoun's antecedent and rewrite each sentence so that the meaning is clear. Assume that gender is correct.

1. The bottle hit the window, and it broke.
   Replace *it* with *the bottle* or *the window*.

2. Hayden checked the numbers and told John that he had won the state lottery.
   Replace *he* with *John* or *Hayden*.

3. The dog chased the cat until he stopped.
   Replace *he* with *the dog* or *the cat*.

4. The department heads told the managers that <u>they</u> needed to give budgetary information to the CEO.
   Replace *they* with *the department heads* or *the managers*.

5. If a corporation disputes the Agency's decision, <u>it</u> must disclose all relevant information.
   Replace *it* with *the corporation* or *the Agency*.

C. Case

If an underlined pronoun is incorrect, replace it with the correct one Assume that gender is correct.

1. Betsy went to lunch with Diane and <u>I</u>.
   Replace *I* with *me*.

2. For <u>who</u> did the bell toll?
   Replace *who* with *whom*.

3. Did the bell toll for <u>she</u> or <u>he</u>?
   Replace *she* with *her* and *he* with *him*.

4. We sent the notice to <u>yours</u> and <u>their</u> attorneys.
   Replace *yours* with *your*; *their* is correct.

5. The letter was sent to Andy and <u>me</u> concerning the person <u>who</u> the Board is considering for the position.
   ***Me* is correct; replace *who* with *whom*.**

6. Mary felt sorry for the lawyer <u>who</u> the judge had held in contempt.
   Replace *who* with *whom*.

7. <u>Who</u> besides <u>he</u> did the seller notify?
   Replace *who* with *whom*; replace *he* with *him*.

8. If <u>they</u> do not get involved, what will happen to <u>he</u> and <u>I</u>?
   ***They* is correct (assuming that *they* refers to multiple people or entities); replace *he* with *him*, and replace *I* with *me*.**

9. <u>Whom</u> was the person <u>who</u> had custody of the dog when it chased my brother and <u>me</u>?
   Replace *whom* with *who*; *who* and *me* are correct.

10 The judge greeted my partner and <u>I</u>.
   Replace *I* with *me*.

IV. PUNCTUATION

A. Spotting Punctuation Errors

Circle any comma, semi-colon, colon, or apostrophe that is <u>incorrectly used</u> in the following sentences:

1. Nancy bought an emerald ring; but she was dissatisfied with it's setting, and returned it.
   The semicolon should be a comma, and there should be no apostrophe in *its*.

2. "I am dissatisfied", Nancy said to the store manager.
   The comma should be placed before the final Quotation mark.

3. Ted bought a novel, and read it in a day.
   Delete the comma.

4. Lindsay drove to the campus, but she could not find a parking spot.
   The comma is correct.

5. Three people spoke at the meeting: Emily, an attorney, Katie, a writer, and Sara, a film director.
   The colon is correct; place a semicolon after *attorney* and after *writer*.

B. Adding Punctuation

Where appropriate, add a comma, semicolon, apostrophe or period. If a sentence requires no additional punctuation, write NPR.

1. During his teenage years, Rod saw only three bands perform on stage: Pink Floyd; The Who; and Led Zeppelin, his favorite band.

2. "You have to go to the dentist," Twyla said to her son; "I don't want to go," the boy replied.
   [*You could replace the semicolon after "son" with a period, breaking the sentence into two sentences.*]

3. After putting away the children's toys, the babysitter fed the dog, made lunch, and settled in front of the TV.
   [*Some people consider the so-called "Oxford Comma" after lunch to be optional.*]

4. "It's a wonderful world," Sandra thought, as she watched her puppy chase its toy.

5. After spending a week in Miami, Victorina went to Madrid, Barcelona, and Paris; she enjoyed her vacation.
   [*Some people consider the so-called "Oxford Comma" after Barcelona to be optional; you could replace the semicolon after Paris with a period, breaking the sentence into two sentences.*]

V. SIMPLICITY AND CONCISENESS

A. Words and Phrases

Write a simpler or more concise substitute for each of the underlined words and phrases.

1. Kathleen spoke <u>in a pleasant manner</u>.
   Kathleen spoke <u>pleasantly</u>.

2. <u>In the event that</u> Cal is sick, he will not go to work.
   <u>If</u> Cal is sick, he will not go to work.

3. Ron wrote the book <u>in conjunction with</u> Harriet.
   Ron wrote the book <u>with</u> Harriet.

4. Caroline <u>made an inquiry</u> about the school's rules.
   Caroline <u>asked</u> about the school's rules.

5. Josh <u>ameliorated</u> his grade by doing extra-credit work.
   Josh <u>improved</u> his grade by doing extra-credit work.

6. Jennifer <u>utilized</u> a computer to write her novel.
   Jennifer <u>used</u> a computer to write her novel.

7. Henry proposed to Rebecca <u>in the month of February</u>.
   Henry proposed to Rebecca <u>in February</u>.

8. Maggie made her car payments <u>on a monthly basis</u>.
   Maggie made her car payments <u>monthly</u>.

9. Joy is driving to the store <u>at the present time</u>.
   Joy is driving to the store <u>now</u>.

10. Scott left his job <u>due to the fact</u> that he hated it.
    Scott left his job <u>because</u> he hated it.

11. The murder trial <u>commenced</u> on Monday.
    The murder trial <u>began</u> on Monday.

12. The City will accept bids <u>subsequent to</u> July 10.
    The City will accept bids <u>after</u> July 10.

13. Cassie went shopping <u>prior to</u> Christmas.
    Cassie went shopping <u>before</u> Christmas.

14. The lion hunted <u>in order to</u> survive.
    The lion hunted <u>to</u> survive.

15. Mick <u>endeavored</u> to write a song.
    Mick <u>tried</u> to write a song.

B. Sentences

Make the following sentences as simple and concise as you can without changing the essence.

1. Gifts were received by Jennifer, on the fifth anniversary of her birth, from her mother and father.
   On her fifth birthday, Jennifer received gifts from her parents.

2. Tracy planned to make a donation, in the form of a monetary contribution, to an organization that was engaged in charitable activities.
   Tracy planned to donate money to a charitable organization.

3. Albert is a man who enjoys reading and has a preference for authors who write concisely by using no more words than are absolutely necessary to convey the intended message.
   Albert enjoys reading and prefers authors who write concisely.

4. Bart served, throughout all of the year 2012, as the chairman of the budget committee of the club, which committee (as suggested by its name) was responsible for dealing with issues relating to the club's budget.
   Throughout 2012, Bart was the chairman of the club's budget committee.

5. Huge bonuses were paid by the company, despite the fact that substantial losses were reported by the company and despite the fact that the company had decided that it was necessary to lay off a significant number of individuals who were employed by the company, to executive-level employees.
   Despite reporting losses and deciding to lay off employees, the company paid huge bonuses to executives.

SELECTED BIBLIOGRAPHY

The Bluebook: A Uniform System of Citation. 19th ed. Cambridge, MA: Harvard Law Review Association, 2010.

Fowler, H. Ramsey. *The Little Brown Handbook.* 2nd. ed. Boston: Little, Brown and Company, 1983.

Fowler, H. W. *A Dictionary of Modern Usage.* 2nd ed. Revised and edited by Sir Ernest Gowers. New York: Oxford University Press, 1965.

Garner, Bryan A. *The Redbook: A Manual on Legal Style.* St. Paul: West Group, 2002.

Glenn, Cheryl, and Loretta Gray. *The Hodges Harbrace Handbook.* 18th ed. Boston: Wadsworth, 2012.

Hacker, Diana. *The Bedford Handbook: Instructor's Annotated Edition.* 5th ed. Boston: Bedford Books, 1998.

Hodges, John C. *Harbrace College Handbook.* 4th ed. New York: Harcourt, Brace and Company, 1956.

---. *Harbrace Handbook of English.* 1st ed. New York: Harcourt, Brace and Company, 1941.

Kirszner, Laura G., and Stephen R. Mandell. *The Holt Handbook.* 6th ed. Fort Worth: Harcourt, 2002.

Loberger, Gordon, and Kate Shoup. *Webster's New World English Grammar Handbook.* 2nd ed. Hoboken: Wiley, 2009.

New Oxford American Dictionary. 2nd ed. Edited by Erin McKean. New York: Oxford University Press, 2005.

Strunk, William, Jr., and E. B. White, *The Elements of Style.* 50th Anniversary Ed. New York: Pearson Longman, 2009

---. *The Elements of Style.* 3rd Ed. New York: MacMillan Publishing, 1979.

University of Chicago Press. *The Chicago Manual of Style: The Essential Guide for Writers, Editors and Publishers.* 15th ed. Chicago: University of Chicago Press, 2003.

Warriner, John E. *English Grammar and Composition.* Franklin Ed. New York: Harcourt Brace Jovanovich, 1982.

Zinsser, William. *On Writing Well: The Classic Guide to Writing Nonfiction.* 30th Anniversary Ed. New York: HarperCollins, 2006.

INDEX